In the chur, pagan practices were adopted into the early church for much the same reason as Christianity is being watered down today; to make God's Word more palatable to those outside who otherwise would not accept it and to fill up the pews. However, once God's Word has been added to or taken away from, it ceases to be the Word of God and it becomes yet another tradition of man.

Robert Cook has extensively researched the Bible and the writings of the early church to expose to the reader man-made doctrines that now seem to form much of the theology currently espoused by virtually all Christian denominations and non-denominational Christian churches. Anyone who considers themselves to be a Christian should certainly reconsider their beliefs as they pertain to these and other false teachings that are so abundant at small country churches and big city mega-churches alike.

Throughout *The Jerusalem Church: Learn Not the Way of the Heathen*, Mr. Cook provides the reader with chapter and verse references so that his analysis of a topic can be checked out in God's word (as all works of men should be). After reading this book and following up with the appropriate prayerful study of the Bible, I have no doubt that the reader will be blessed with a greater understanding of the Word.

—Derek Burton,
Environmental Scientist and Project Manager

—THE—
JERUSALEM CHURCH

— THE —
JERUSALEM CHURCH
LEARN NOT THE WAY OF THE HEATHEN

ROBERT COOK

TATE PUBLISHING & *Enterprises*

Published by Tate Publishing & Enterprises, LLC
127 E. Trade Center Terrace | Mustang, Oklahoma 73064 USA
1.888.361.9473 | www.tatepublishing.com

Tate Publishing is committed to excellence in the publishing industry. The company reflects the philosophy established by the founders, based on Psalm 68:11,
"The Lord gave the word and great was the company of those who published it."

Book design copyright © 2009 by Tate Publishing, LLC. All rights reserved.
Cover design by Kandi Evans
Interior design by Joey Garrett

Published in the United States of America

ISBN: 978-1-61566-546-4
Religion / Christian Theology / General
09.11.20

Table of Contents

Introduction

"Learn not the way of the heathen" is the beginning of a specific message from God in Jeremiah 10:1–5 (KJV) to his people about pagan ritual, and in the Bible, the word *heathen* always speaks of a people not included among the family of God. Throughout time, pagan ritual and worship have crept into the worship of God, and for a time, God will leave it on the shoulders of men to do something about it. But when men refuse or simply don't do anything about it, God will step in and take care of it on his own. Unfortunately, when God steps in to do what man was supposed to do but didn't, it brings tribulation because allowing pagan ritual or worship to continue within the family of God is an act of negligence on the part of man.

There are those who would want us to believe that ignorance is bliss, but the Bible clearly tells us in 2 Timothy 2:15, 16, "Study (the word of God) to show yourselves approved (one who is a proven servant of Christ) to God, a workman (laborer) that is not ashamed, rightly dividing the word. But shun profane and vain babblings: for they will increase into more ungodliness" (KJV). In verse 15, the words *rightly dividing* are used to speak of someone who teaches the truth correctly and directly, which means teaching the Word of God just as God meant it to be preached, whether it is hard or soft. So by these Scriptures, we can see that if we claim to be a member of the family of God, but if we don't study the Word of God, then we are living in rebellion against the commandment to study his Word. It is the responsibility of all members of the body of Christ to research and study the Word of God so that we will know what is written and what is not written in his Word. This means that ignorance is not an excuse for being disobedient.

God has given me a heart for his people, an unquenchable desire to study and research his word, and a passion to preach his Word as I have discovered it. For these reasons I have written this book in an effort to show the family of God what I have found.

ROBERT COOK

Doctrinal Beliefs:

What Doctrines Did the Early Church Believe In?

To better we understand what is happening today with the church and world events, it is most important that we know and understand how the early church was, what they believed, and how they lived.

There is no doubt the Jerusalem church which was the first seat of Christian authority was influenced by Judaism, the beliefs of the Pharisees and certain aspects or customs of Jewish life. We also need to understand that Judaism was a way of life for the Israelites before Christ came along and that most of the early church members were Jewish.

We must understand and accept the fact that the Jewish people are the first people of God, and they hold a special place in the heart of God, whether they are disobedient or not. We need to understand how God feels about the Jewish people by understanding what the Bible says about them. They are the apple of his eye.

In Romans 1:16, Paul is writing a letter to the church in Rome, which was made up of mostly Gentiles. Here, Paul is speaking of proclaiming the gospel to the Roman church, but he makes it clear they know that the salvation of God is for the Jew first and then for the Gentile. In chapter 2, verses 9 and 10, Paul speaks of how tribulation and anguish will come to those who do evil to the Jew first and also to the Gentile. To all of who do evil against all who are the people of God, though the gospel was preached to the Jew first we are all now included in the family of God. In Romans 11:17, 24, Paul is telling the Gentiles that we are the wild (untamed) olive trees that are grafted in among the tamed and cultivated olive trees. In this verse, the Jews call the wild olive tree "Oleaster tree." The tree's more common name is the Russian olive tree. It grows from between twelve and forty-five feet tall and can grow as many as six feet in one year. The tree has small aromatic yellow flowers, the leaves are covered with a scale like substance that gives them the appearance of silvery scales and the fruit, a small cherry-like drupe, are edible and sweet. But the Oleaster tree is considered to be an invasive species because of its low seedling mortality rates and its ability to consume areas of ground.

Russian olive trees have no foliage value for livestock or big game. They interfere with agricultural practices by rapidly colonizing lowland fields, choking irrigation ditches, damaging tires of farming equipment, and are considered to be a noxious weed.

Like the Oleaster tree in the days of Jesus, the gentiles were not considered to be worthy of much more than slaves, but God, through his grace, has given the gentile the same rank and acceptance as the Israelite. But since we have been grafted in among and with the naturally cultivated olive trees, we are partakers of the root and fatness of the cultivated olive trees.

Since the beginning, God has always accepted any and all persons who wanted to convert to Judaism and

ROBERT COOK

believe in the one true, living God. There are many people written about in the Bible who were not of a Jewish bloodline who were blessed by God and used by God to accomplish his will and who were worthy of being written about in the Bible. They were people like Rahab, the harlot who helped the two men Joshua sent out to spy on the land and the city of Jericho. Because of what she did, not only was she saved, but her family that was with her when Jericho was destroyed was also saved. After the city was destroyed, they went with the Israelites and later were provided with land to settle on.

There is Ruth, who was a Moabite woman (a Gentile) whose Jewish mother-in-law, Naomi, told her to go back to her mother's house after Ruth lost her husband. But Ruth refused to leave the side of her mother-in-law and went with her back to Israel. After she got there, she ended up marrying a rich, well-respected Israelite man named Boaz. It was at that point that Ruth became an important member of the bloodline that would lead through David on down to Joseph, who was the husband of Mary, who gave birth to Christ. Ruth and Rahab are just two examples of converts in the Old Testament.

In the book of Revelation, the first church spoken of is the Church of Ephesus, and while it is true there is a place called by that name and there was a church there, it is the meaning of the word *Ephesus* that is more important. It means desirable one, and it is the church that Jesus desires to eat with at the wedding supper. The complaint that Jesus had against them was the result of too much focus on the ministry and not enough focus on Christ, who was their first love. They loved one another, they helped one another, and their basic mind-set was that of a brotherhood. They had true fellowship with each other. Today I cannot think of any denominational or nondenominational church that has that kind of close relationship. I do know of or have seen small pockets or groups within a group that have that kind of relationship such as a singles ministry, a youth ministry, a woman's or maybe a men's ministry. But for the most part the church as a whole is void of the kind of close relationship like the first church had. Their services did not have a set structure, and anyone could participate. They would read and explain the Scriptures just like was done in the synagogues, and then they would have common prayer, praise, and worship. They would have what was called an *agape* (the unconditional love of God), or *love feast*, where they would break bread, fellowship, take communion, and worship the Lord together. The origin of this love feast was, of course, the Last Supper with Jesus right before he was crucified. The Last Supper started this tradition, and it lasted until sometime in the latter part of the first century. They would have church at their homes, and as their numbers grew, they would remodel to make room for the church growth. They usually either had a baptistery or would baptize converts in a river or the sea, and they believed in total body immersion. The leaders of these congregations were often a group of elders or bishops, and they had a board of deacons who would do the practical jobs. They swept floors, washed eating utensils, and any number of other menial tasks. They were considered to be servants and nothing even remotely close to what deacons are considered today. In this day and age, deacons are considered to be, in many cases, great men of respect who dictate how and on what to spend church money on. In most cases they

ROBERT COOK

lord over the pastor and are considered to be too good to clean a toilet or mop a floor.

These leaders were chosen from among the congregation and were seated in the front. They had four styles of preaching that fit into the five-fold ministry. There was the evangelistic preaching, which spoke of the fundamentals of the Christian message, the teaching style, which clarified the meanings, importance, and the understanding of that which had been proclaimed, and the exhortation style, which was preached to build up the congregation and served also as the prophetic office to urge and tell the congregation to take on the obligation to structure and conform their lives to that of a Christian lifestyle. The rules and regulations of the church were done via the democratic process. Decisions were made according to the majority vote and the prophetic witness and the deacons were simply part of the whole voting group. There were no clergy or laity, and deacons, the elders and bishops were considered to be servants who did nothing else but serve the members of the congregation and purposes of God, unlike today when so many high-profile pastors with huge mega churches who have the time to manage personal businesses and enterprises as well as church business. Scripturally speaking, pastors who are in right relationship with God have no time to do anything else except their God-job.

There is nothing wrong with a pastor having a job outside of managing a church but the bigger the church the less time a pastor should have to focus on his own business. In short the pastor of a mega-church or even a church with only a few thousand members shouldn't have any time to focus on making himself money and the church should be providing for his living needs.

The Romans had several well-kept highways throughout their empire, so travel from city to city was easy for the most part, which made it easier for missionaries to travel and spread the gospel. They would meet on a certain day just before dawn and sing an anthem to Christ as God and swear an oath to abstain from stealing, sexual immorality, fraud, never to commit wicked deeds, and to be persons of integrity who could be trusted to honor their word always, unlike these days when internationally known pastors fall from grace with a loud thud. After this, they would go about their daily business and meet again later for the agape feast.

In Acts 2:41–47 (KJV), the Bible says that after the new converts were baptized, they would continue steadfastly to give constant attention to their new life with God and their fellow servants in Christ. They had all things in common; they had one mind with one accord, and they sold their possessions, their goods, and gave them to all men as every man had need of. They continued daily with one accord (one state of mind) in the temple and breaking bread daily from house to house, and they did eat their meal with gladness and singleness of heart, praising God and having favor with all people. This was how they had what we now call church. We know from the writings of Paul that false doctrinal teachings were being preached by certain people, but the Bible doesn't speak of any false teachings or divisions within the church until it is encountered in 1 Corinthians, which was written about A.D. 57. This does not mean that there were no false doctrinal teachings before A.D. 57. It just means that the first biblically recorded incident is in 1 Corinthians.

The early church of the first 300 years after the

ROBERT COOK

death of Christ was an innocent church with no false or unscriptural doctrinal teaching because all of their doctrines came from either the apostles who were taught by Christ and the holy spirit or the disciples of the apostles so the word was still fresh, unspoiled and uncorrupted. As I researched the early church, I found that the Christianity of that day was focused mainly on having a relationship with Christ. It was more spiritual than carnal, and it was obedient, had an intimate loving relationship with Christ. They had clear doctrinal teachings that were strictly based on the literal interpretation of the teachings of Jesus and the writings of the apostles. Together they were what made up 90% of the new testament in the first 80 years after the death of Christ. Only the books of Jude and Revelation were written after 80 A.D. They even had a messianic seal that represented the Jerusalem church. It was from the top to the bottom, the seven candlestick menorah, the Star of David, and a fish. The menorah

THE JERUSALEM CHURCH

represents the anointing, and the fish represents the Christians. As you can see, they are interconnected to form the star of David in the middle which represents the whole of the people of God. The seal and what it represented became lost and stayed hidden until sometime in the 1960s when an elderly monk who lived as a hermit in the old city of Jerusalem, whose name was Tech Otecus, found the symbol etched on about forty pieces of artifacts (pottery) excavated from an ancient grotto located somewhere in the vicinity of the upper room on Mount Zion. The notion that the church has replaced the Jewish people as the people of God who are in covenant relationship with God is totally against scriptural teaching and is not spoken of anywhere in the Bible. The fact of the matter is that all Christians should support the Jewish people because they still carry the favor of God whether they are believers of Christ or not. All present and future prophecy revolves around the Jewish state, and it is a new Jerusalem that God and the Lamb will be living in for an eternity with us.

Today, a very large portion of the body of Christ believes in a concept called eternal salvation; it is the belief that once a person gets saved, he will always be saved, no matter what that person does from that point on. If that person lives a pious or virtuous life until he or she dies, he or she would still be saved and will receive eternal life with Christ. If that person, after being saved, begins again to live a life of unrepentant sin until the day, he or she dies, never asking for forgiveness or turning from his or her evil ways, he or she will still receive eternal life with Christ, even if he or she becomes a mass murderer, a rapist, a child molester, a drug addict, or lives the rest of his or her life in sexual immorality.

The doctrinal teaching of eternal salvation, or once saved, always saved, guarantees that a person will still get to spend eternity with Christ instead of living in eternal hell for living in unrepentant sin. But the early church had no such beliefs and did not abide by such nonbiblical concepts as eternal salvation, and they were wise not to believe in that which is not scripturally or morally sound.

Before we move on, I need to point out that in the church world of today there are many new Bible translations taken from the old manuscripts, and for the sake of argument, I will not single out any particular Bible version negatively, but I want to express my feelings about all of these new Bible translations.

There is the Jerusalem Bible, the Vulgate, the Hebrew and Greek manuscripts, a gender neutral Bible, a homosexual Bible, the Catholic Bible, the KJV, the Geneva Bible and so on. Then we have all of the revised versions of the King James Version of the Bible, the Episcopal version, the AMS version, the New American Bible, Samual Lloyds version, the Wycliffe Bible, the ESV, the Darby Bible, the New Living translation, the Douay-Rheims version, the Message Bible—and I could go on and on. Then we have all of those versions of the Bible that are full of the interpretations and notes and commentaries of so many men who claim to be interpreting Scripture correctly just as God intended for his word to be understood. Each one claims to be right. We have the Thompson, the Nelson, the Scolfield, the Jack Van Impe Prophecy Bible, the John C. Hagee Prophecy Bible, and again I could go on, but there is no need. In spite of the claims of accuracy all of these bible versions are so different that two people can disagree on what a particular verse is telling us for no other reason than the fact that one version of the Bible has change one word in that verse as compared to the other version of the Bible being use by the other disagreeing party. The word "axe" that has been changed to the word "chisel." Or the words "breach of promise" that have been removed from that verse and replaced with the one word "opposition." Or the word "Hades" being changed to the word "hell." An axe is not used for the same reason or to do the same kind of work that a chisel is used for. One uses an axe with two hands and cuts down trees, lope limbs off and to split logs with and a chisel is struck with a hammer to carve small pieces of wood away from a chunk of wood for the purpose of making art. Both words are a long ways from each other but somehow there are Bible versions whose authors or translators have seen fit to replace the word "axe" with the word "chisel." So we have two people telling each other what the Bible says or doesn't say in the process of disagreement and both of them are right. However only one version or neither version of the bibles they are studying from are correct. Therefore our understanding of the word of God has been confounded.

In the long run all of these so called accurate Bible translations and interpretations are causing massive confusion and discord within the body of Christ. False interpretations of what the Bible is telling us have caused large denominational splits and rifts. The church of today is very much divided with very little unity on many eternally significant issues and doctrinal beliefs thanks to all of these bible translations.

The question is. Is this what God intended for us

to do with his word? Most of these Bible translations were done for the reason of making the word of God easier to understand but in reality the word of God has been corrupted. Even the King James version has words that were change in the interest of making it easier to understand the word of God.

So which Bible would be the right or best bible to study from?

Since the English, the Hebrew and the Greek languages have changed over time and Bible versions have been changed to accommodate these language changes. I believe that the best way to study the word of God is to use the oldest versions of the English Bible that we can find, along with the oldest study guilds such as lexicons and dictionaries. I never use any commentaries because they are yet another man's opinion who may or may not have been influenced by a false doctrinal teaching, idea, belief or concept. In any case I try to remain as mentally pure as it is possible when it comes to biblical research.

The only English version of the Hebrew and Greek manuscripts that has stood the test of time is the King James Version of 1611. It has been the number one selling Bible for almost 400 years and has been translated into nearly every language known to man. The only reason this Bible version and the revised version of 1629 has been at the top for so long is because it has been blessed by God. God saw to it that this Bible version has been the main stay of Bible versions since King James commissioned it to be done.

For these reasons, it is the King James Version of 1611 that I choose to use as my main source of biblical research for this book.

Most who disagree with me do so because they are

using a different more modern Bible translation so I would challenge anyone who disagrees with me to do the research. Don't simply take my word for it. Do the research and find out for yourself if what I say is correct or wrong.

Hell:

Where and What Is It?

In the English Bible, the word we know of as hell is the word *sheol* in the Hebrew and is considered to be the abode or house of the dead. In the Greek, the word hell means "the place of the dead." The early church believed that Hades was the place where the souls of those who have departed from this life abide, both the righteous and the wicked. The place of *sheol* consists of two sections: one is for the wicked and is a place of burning and torment, which was known as Gahanna; the other section is for the righteous and is a place of rest, which is also known as paradise or the bosom of Abraham. There are those who teach that when we die, we go straight to heaven, but there is no scriptural proof of that happening to anybody in the Bible. Enoch and Elijah never tasted of the stench of death, and when Jesus died, the first place he went was to paradise or the bosom of Abraham, where he spent three days and nights preaching to all who were in Hades before he walked or transported himself around on this earth for forty days before being taken up to heaven, which is the abode of God and of his Son only. We know that when Christ willingly gave himself on the cross, he died for all sins and sinners, present and those of the future and the past sins of those who were considered to be Old Testament saints or righteous people. This is why Jesus had to first descend into the lower reaches of the earth so he could proclaim the good news to both the righteous and the wicked. On resurrection day, paradise will give up all of those who are considered to be righteous in the eyes of God through the shed blood of Christ, but the wicked and the Old Testament saints will remain until the great white throne judgment. These beliefs are in part a rollover from Judaism, and by studying Old Testament Jewish customs and beliefs, we can help ourselves better understand what the New Testament is explaining to us.

ROBERT COOK

The Mark of the Beast:
How They Would Recognize It

There are many different theories and speculations as to the identity of the man of sin or the beast out in the church world these days, and because everybody insists he or she is right and everybody else's theories are wrong, it leads to much confusion about end time prophecy, especially in regard to the mark of the beast. The plain fact of the matter is that God never intended for there to be so much confusion about his prophetic word and it is that confusion which leads millions of his people to simply shun any discussion or teaching or studying the very word that our Lord and Savior has commanded us to study so that we may be approved of by the Father. What most Christians do is simply take the word of their pastor, teacher, or expert in the field of prophecy as if it were the truth without ever doing some research for themselves to find out if their pastor or Bible teacher or those who claim to be an expert in the field of biblical prophecy are actually teaching what the Bible says exactly as the Bible says it. However the writings of the early Christians have no confusion as to what the phrase "the number of his name" is speaking of.

Both the Romans and the Greeks had an alphabetical system that was also used as their numbering system, so the early Christians knew that it would be the alphabetical letters in the antichrist's name that would tell them who he really was, and it was not something out of the ordinary to them. Whatever the name of the man of sin might be, its spelling will equal the number 666.

Because of their Jewish heritage, another bit of knowledge that most all of the early Christian writers were aware of is that the number 666 first shows up in the Old Testament. First Kings 10:14 says, "Now the weight of gold that came to Solomon in one year was six hundred three score (a score is 20) and six talents of gold" (KJV). This makes up the number 666. In Revelation 13:18, John the Revelator writes, "Here is wisdom. Let him that has understanding count the number of the beast: for it is the number of a man; and that number is six hundred three score and six." We must remember that the original New Testament manuscripts were written in Greek. The Old Testament was written in Hebrew, and the Hebrews also had a numbering system. It is not a coincidence that both times the number six hundred three score and six has been written in both the Old Testament and the New Testament in exactly the same way, and both times, the number 666 is spoken of in relation to money. Could this be a clue to the identity of the antichrist?

Other than the written word itself, there doesn't seem to be much that was put to pen and paper until after the first century about the mark of the beast. Hippolytus, who was born in A.D. 170, and an early church leader became one of the most prolific writers of the early church. He was a priest in the Church of Rome who was known for extensive and profound teaching. His greatest work was "The Apostolic Tradition" which was a glimpse liturgical and devotional life of Roman Christians around the year 200 A.D. It is simply amazing to me that a man who lived 1,800 years ago was able to pen these words:

> (The antichrist) will order censers to be set up by everyone, everywhere, so that no one among the saints may be able to buy or sell without first sacrificing. For this is what is meant by the mark received upon the right hand. And the phrase, "on their forehead," indicates that all are crowned. That is, put on a crown of fire. This is the crown of death, not of life.

When Hippolytus wrote about these censers, he had no way of knowing just how close he was to the futuristic reality of what one day will be in our lives. Though Hippolytus was talking about pinching a little incense to be burned in a censer the choice to choose between the things of this world and the things of God are the same. Our choice will be to sacrifice our soul to eternal death or live in a world dominated by ungodliness. Today, we have microchips with lithium batteries that are stored inside a small glass tube and can be injected into the body using a syringe. The microchip can be programmed to store information such as identity, medical records, criminal records, and most importantly, financial records. Once the chip is inserted, there are sensors that can be posted at any door or opening to or in any building or place of business. These sensors send out a signal that causes the microchip to give up the information it carries, which means that before one walks past any censer, all or at least part of the information stored in the microchip is monitored by someone else. In other words, before you walk in the door, they already know who you are, what bank you use, and how much money you have.

There is also an ink that has been developed by a company out of St. Louis, Missouri, that can hold information just like the microchip and can be prompted to give the information held in the ink. The ink has already been put on the hide of cattle using the same process used for tattooing.

The Great Tribulation and the Resurrection of the Dead:

How Did They Feel About Tribulations?

We must remember that the early Christian writers were first-, second-, and third-century Christians who were taught by Jesus, the disciples of Jesus, their disciples, and so on. This means there were very few corrupt scriptural interpretations and even fewer false doctrinal teachings. Many of those early Christian writers had some of their own opinions about some of the most complicated and least understood prophetic Scriptures, but they would never fully understand many of those prophetic scriptures in the New Testament unless they lived for two thousand years, watching them being fulfilled. To them, everything prophetic in the New Testament was to be fulfilled in the future.

There was no such thing as a pre-tribulation resurrection concept in the early church because they interpreted the Bible literally, and they were very careful not to stray from the teachings of Christ and his apostles. Whenever outsiders came and tried to bring in a false belief, they would speak out against these false doctrinal teachings and even run those teaching those corruptions slap out of the church.

Irenaeus, who was born in A.D. 125, lived in Ephesus, which is now part of Turkey, where he heard the preaching of Polycarp, who was a student of the Apostle John. One of the passions Irenaeus had was fighting against heresies within the church, and one of the earliest heresies to come into the church was Gnosticism. Gnostics believe that there are two opposing forces: light against darkness, good against evil, and so on. They denied that God had created the earth; they taught that Christ did not really have a material body, that Jesus was not really born, that Jesus did not actually suffer and die, and they believed that they were the spiritually elite and closer to the truth than any other group, just to mention a few false teachings. In opposition to false teaching, Irenaeus taught that the gospel was for everyone, spoke of the church as being universal, and his principal work was called *Against Heresies*, which has five volumes in defense of orthodox Christianity against the Gnostics.

The early church believed that the great tribulation was going to be a contest or test of the righteous, and Irenaeus wrote, "There will be tribulation such as has not been since the beginning, neither will be. For this is the last contest of the righteous, in which they are crowned with incorruption when they overcome." Another early church leader named Hippolytus wrote: "The woman was given two wings of the great eagle, so that she could fly into the wilderness, where she is nourished for a time, and times, and half a time, from the face of the serpent' (Revelation 12:14, KJV). That refers to the 1,260 days during which the tyrant is to reign and persecute the church, which flees from city to city, and seeks concealment in the wilderness among the mountains. She possesses no other defense then the two wings of the great eagle, that is to say, the faith of Jesus Christ." It is important to note here that at the time of this writing, there was no such a thing as the country or state of Israel. After the destruction of Jerusalem and the temple in A.D. 70, the Romans wanted to wipe the memory of the Israelite people from the face of the earth, so they changed the name of the country from Israel to what we now know as Palestine. However, today the Israelite people have returned to the land that God gave to them, and through several declarations and short wars, they have inhabited the land and changed the name of the land back to Israel. So at the time of Hippolytus, the only entity that could fit the description on the woman in chapter 12 of the book of Revelation could only have been the church.

Today, we know that the only country that can fit the description of the woman can be none other than Israel. The number twelve in the Bible always represents governmental perfection, and the original tribal leaders from the twelve tribes that made up the Israelite people were the government of Israel with Moses at the head as a type of intercessor. The crown of twelve stars on the woman's head signifies royalty, and each star represents one of the twelve tribes of Israel.

The most important facts here are the time, times, and halftimes, which equals 1,260 days which equals three and one half years. Early Christian writers got it right. There is nothing written anywhere in the Bible that says anything about any seven years of tribulation. The Bible speaks of a period of seven years in which there will be a period of tribulation and a period of the wrath of God. The wrath of God and tribulation are not the same.

Victorinus wrote several well-known and scholarly commentaries on the Old and New Testament, but unfortunately only a few scraps of his works about Genesis and Revelation have survived. He fought against several of the heresies of his time, and he believed that Christ would return to earth and rule for a thousand years, which was later condemned as heresy by the church at Rome, which is why many of his works were suppressed and lost. However, today, we know that he was right, and Christ will be returning to reign for one thousand years. It is also believed that he was the first to have done writings written in Latin by a Christian. He died a martyr's death under the persecutions of the Roman emperor Diocletian sometime in A.D. 303 or 304.

Victorinus also believed that the three and one half year mark would be a turning point for the world. He wrote, "When the three years and six months are completed in the preaching of Elijah, [Satan] will be cast down from heaven. For up until that time he had had the power of ascending. And all the apostate angels, as well as the antichrist, must be roused up from Hades. 'And I saw a beast rising up from the sea like a leopard' (Revelation 13:1, 2, KJV). This signifies the kingdom of that time of the antichrist and the people mingled with the variety of nations."

ROBERT COOK

The Flesh and the
Glorified Body:
What Happens to the Flesh?

The early church believed that since it is the flesh that dies, it will be the flesh that rises from the grave but will be changed to the glorified body after the resurrection if one is judged to be worthy of the glorified body.

Tertullian was a leader in the church and a prolific author of early Christianity. He was born and died in Carthage in what is today called Tunisia. Tertullian spoke out against Christian doctrines he considered to be heretical and was the first great writer of Christian works to be written in Latin, and he introduced the term *trinity*, or in the Latin spelling *trinitas*, to the Christian vocabulary and systematically spoke out against the classical religion of the Roman church and other accepted cults as being superstitions. He was converted to Christianity in about A.D. 197 or 198, and thirty-one of his complete works, along with fragments of more, have survived. His writings cover the whole spectrum of the Christian theological beliefs of his day, which were apologetics against paganism, Judaism, polemics (controversy), polity (church government), discipline, and morals. They give a picture of the religious life and thought processes of his day. Tertullian was the first to cripple such charges that the Christians sacrificed infants at the celebration of the Lord's Supper and committed incest. He pointed out that such crimes existed in the pagan world and then proved that Christians pledged themselves not to commit murder, adultery, or other crimes. Among his apologetic writings is the *Apologeticus*, which was addressed to the Roman magistrates. It is the most piercing defense of Christianity ever written against the reproaches of pagans and one of the magnificent legacies of the ancient church, full of enthusiasm, courage, and vigor. He proclaims the principle of religious freedom as an inalienable right of man and demands a fair trial for the Christians before they are condemned to death. He stated that the gods of the Romans do not exist; therefore, there are no pagan religions against which Christians can offend and that Christians do not engage in the foolishness of the emperors, but they do better by praying for them, and most importantly, he stated that Christians can afford to be put to torture and death in the name of Jesus because the more the church was cast down, the more it grew, which is how the gospel of Christ has spread around the world to where it is today. For without the persecution, the body of Christ would not be what it is today.

Here is what Tertullian had to say about the resurrection of the dead:

> You will also allow that it is the flesh that Christ was raised from the dead. For the very same body that fell in death, and which lay in the sepulcher did rise again. We profess our belief that (the flesh) there in all the grandeur of the Father's

ROBERT COOK

glory. It is therefore just as impossible for us to say that [his flesh] was abolished, as it is for us to maintain that it was sinful. If the flesh is to be repaired after its dissolution, much more will it be restored after some violent injury...is not the amputation or the crushing of a limb? Now, if the death of the whole person is rescinded by its resurrection, what must we say of the death of a part of him...Accordingly, for a dead man to be raised again, amounts to nothing short of his being restored to his entire condition. Otherwise, he would still be dead in that part in which he has not risen again. God is quite capable of remaking what He once made. He who has already traveled through Hades is destined to obtain the change after the resurrection. It is from this circumstance that we definitively declare that the flesh will by all means rise again. Because of the change that is to come over it, it will assume the condition of the angels.

THE JERUSALEM CHURCH

Going to Heaven:
Where Do We Go When We Die and When?

The early church did not believe in any way, shape, or form the idea of going to heaven as soon as we die, and if one would do some biblical research, one would find that there is not one single Scripture that speaks of going straight to heaven on the day we die, and if the Bible doesn't speak of it, then it is not. When we die, we either go to the place of burning or we go to paradise, and both of these realms exist in Hades.

> "We maintain that after life has passed away you still remain in existence and anticipate a Day of Judgment. (In the Judgment), according to your deserts, (deeds) you are assigned to misery or to bliss. Either way, it will be forever. To be capable of this, your former substance must return to you the matter (body) and memory of the very same human being. For if you were not endowed with that sensitive bodily organization, you could fell neither good nor evil. And there would be no grounds for judgment without the presentation of the very person to whom the sufferings of judgment were due."
>
> —Origen

Another gifted Christian writer was considered to be one of the greatest Christian theologians of his time and before. His name was Origen, and he was born in A.D. 185 or 186. Origen was not quit seventeen when the Roman Emperor Septimius Severus began a Christian persecution. Origen lived during a turbulent time when there were periodic Christian persecutions during the reigns of Emperors Severus, Maximin, and Decius. Also during his time, the Roman Empire was threatened with destabilization because of the barbarian invasions that were sweeping across Europe. He was born into great Christian persecution, and he died sometime in 254 or 255 while still living under great Christian persecution. In Origen's time, Christianity had not yet established a system of theological beliefs as a basis of orthodoxy, so there were several different sects, and each one claimed to posses the truth about the Christian faith. The largest of the different sects were the Gnostics, and it is the Gnostic doctrine that Origen fought hardest against. Since there were no non-Gnostic theological systems that were as successful as the Gnostics in his day, Origen formulated one. Because of Origin, his works and the works of many other wise theologians like him, much of what we believe today is a direct result of their efforts to keep paganism and false doctrinal teachings out of the body of Christ. However, after these dedicated men had all passed away and the church became organized with the seat of Christian authority being transferred from Jerusalem to the church at Rome, there were several false doctrinal beliefs, and many pagan rituals that crept back into the church. Men like Origen were instrumental in the fight against pagan worship and left-field concepts like Gnosticism.

ROBERT COOK

Like several other early church theologians, Origen also wrote.

> Ignorant men (uneducated believers) and unbelievers suppose that our flesh is destroyed after death to such a degree that it retains no relic at all of its former substance. However, we who believe in its resurrection understand that only a change has been produced by death. … It will again be raised from the earth. And after this it will advance to the glory of a spiritual body according to the merits of the indwelling soul. We are to believe, then, that all this bodily substance will be brought into this condition. This will be when all things will be re-established into a state of unity and when God will be "all in all" And this result must be understood as being brought about, not suddenly but slowly [in process of time] and gradually.

It also seems that Origen contradicts himself. "The apostolic teaching is that there is to be a time of resurrection from the dead, when the body which now is sown in corruption will rise in incorruption; and when that which "is sown in dishonor will rise in glory." We know now that the flesh will not rise from the grave just as it went into the grave and even if it did, changing into the glorified body on the way up to heaven accomplishes the same task. Anyway, believing that the flesh will rise from the grave just before it changes into the glorified body is not eternally significant.

This belief shows that the believers of the early church not only did not believe in the ascension to heaven at the moment of death but believed we go into the earth and stay there until we are called by Jesus to come forth from the grave. Again, the early church got it right because there is not one single word in the Bible that tells us that we will go to heaven immediately after the moment of death.

There are those who would argue against this concept of not going to heaven when we die and as always the words "To be absent from the body is to be present with the Lord" are used to argue against it. However this is a major blunder when the rest of the words for this verse are left un-said. When quoting this partial verse it does without a doubt confound a true understanding of what this verse actually says and leads the believer to think that we actually do go straight to heaven as soon as We die. But 2 Corinthians 5:8 does not say that.

It says, "We are confident, I say, (and willing rather) to be absent from the body, and to be present with the Lord." This verse is not telling us that if we die we will go directly to heaven to be with Jesus because we are absent from the body. This verse is telling us that we are willing to be absent from our bodies and to be in heaven with Jesus.

So when the words "willing rather" are omitted when quoting from 2 Corinthians 5:8, the entire meaning of the verse is corrupted into saying something that it does not. Indeed I am *willing rather* to be absent from my body and to be in heaven with Jesus, but I am not. How is it that so many can read this verse and miss or not see the two words that bring clarity to the meaning of this verse?

A Childlike Trust
and Persecution:

How Much Faith and Love for One
Another Did They Have?

Polycarp is a prominent figure in the history of the early church. As a pupil of the Apostle John, he lived between the years of A.D. 60 and A.D. 155, a time when there were some apostles who were still alive teaching students who are now considered to be early church leaders. There is not much known about Polycarp before he arrived on the early church scene already a Christian. It is believed that a wealthy woman who was renowned for her gift of giving, whose name was Callisto and was a member of the church of Smyrna, claimed that she had a dream from God that instructed her to go to the Ephesian gate of the city of Ephesus and redeem a young boy who was the slave of two men. So she went and bought Polycarp his freedom, brought him to her home, and raised him with a Christian upbringing. He became a deacon in the church and labored to comfort the poor (oppressed). There was great persecution at the time, so the work of a deacon was quite extensive. They had to care for the women and children of those who were imprisoned or killed. They visited those saints who were in prison to exhort and comfort the suffering saints by bringing them food, clothing, and salves for the lacerations on their backs which came from being lashed, and the only way to get money to pay for some of these creature comforts was to get them from the congregation, who, as a result of the persecution, had very little because of the prejudices and persecutions. Polycarp was soon called to be an elder in the church and after that became pastor and minister (servant) to the church.

He taught that we should remain strong in our faith and flee from materialism. Polycarp was, for a time, the bishop of the church of Smyrna. He was one of the first combatants of Christian heresies such as Gnosticism, paganism, and other false doctrinal teachings that were always trying to creep into the church. He believed that whoever did not confess that Jesus Christ had come in the flesh was antichrist and whoever did not acknowledge the testimony of the cross was of the devil and whoever twisted the sayings of the Lord to suit his own sinful desires and claimed that there was neither resurrection nor judgment, that person was the firstborn of Satan.

> "Therefore, let us leave behind the worthless speculation of the crowd and their false teachings, and let us return to the word delivered to us from the beginning. Let us be self-controlled with respect to prayer and persevere in fasting, earnestly asking the all-seeing God to "lead us not into temptation" because, as the Lord said, "The spirit is indeed willing, but the flesh is weak."
>
> —Polycarp

ROBERT COOK

The single greatest contribution he gave to Christianity was giving up his life to be martyred in the name of the Jesus. His sacrifice is one of the most well-documented events of all of the others who sacrificed their lives for doing what Christ required, which was standing fast in faith no matter what the circumstances were. Polycarp was arrested and taken before a proconsul in Rome simply for being a Christian. At the time, Christianity was considered to be a politically dangerous cult, and its rapid expansion needed to be crushed. So the Roman government had set out to kill this evil cult. The Romans believed that the Christian religion made the local gods angry because of what was considered to be an unrighteous lifestyle. The Roman proconsul asked Polycarp to proclaim, "Caesar is Lord," and offer just a pinch of incense to Caesar's statue, and if he did this, he would escape being tortured and put to death. This is how Polycarp responded:

> Eighty-six years I have served Christ, and He never did me any wrong. How can I blaspheme my king who saved me? You threaten the fire that burns for an hour and then is quenched; but you know not of the fire of the judgment to come, and the fire of eternal punishment. Bring what you will.

Polycarp refused to compromise his beliefs or give up Christ as Lord of all, so they tied him to a large stake and burned him alive until he was dead. He was faithful even unto death, and in the midst of his sacrifice, he received eternal life.

As I said before, the members of the early church had a completely different attitude toward persecution than we have now. They had a profound childlike trust in God, and they practiced a literal and blind obedience to the early teachings of Jesus and the apostles. They didn't question commandments before they would obey them, and they trusted that God's way was always the best way. They trusted God because they lived in awe of his majesty and power.

Felix Marcus Minucius, who was a Christian lawyer and an apologist who practiced in the Roman judicial system, put it like this:

> God is greater than all our perceptions, he is infinite, immense. Only he truly understands his true greatness; our hearts are too limited to really understand him. We are making a worthy estimation of him when we say that he is beyond estimation and anyone who thinks he knows the magnitude of God, diminishes his greatness.

One undeniable indicator of their absolute trust in God was their acceptance of persecution. For approximately two hundred and fifty years, they suffered intermittent persecutions, and they were willing to suffer unspeakable horrors and death at the hands of their persecutors rather than disown the Lord God Almighty. It was their lifestyle and their most effective evangelistic tool. We must remember that God is in total and complete control of everything. He either lets it happen or he makes it happen. But whatever he sends or lets come into our lives, we must always glorify him under any circumstances.

Whenever local persecution stuck its ugly head up, most Christians tried to flee but were against any mass exodus from the Roman Empire. They were convinced that their Father would not let the church be killed and let the Romans know that God alone would preserve the church in spite of their efforts to kill it.

Origen spoke this to the Romans:

> When God gives the Tempter permission to persecute us, we suffer persecution. And when God wishes us to be free from suffering, even though surrounded by a world that hates us, we enjoy a wonderful peace. We trust in the protection of the one who said, 'Be of good cheer, for I have overcome the world.' And truly he has overcome the world. Therefore, the world prevails only as long as it is permitted to by him who received power from the Father to overcome the world. From his victory we take courage. Even if he should again wish us to suffer and contend for our faith, let the enemy come against us. We will say to them, 'I can do all things through Christ Jesus our Lord who strengthens me.'

Origen also told the Romans point blank, "Eventually, every form of worship will be destroyed except the religion of Christ, which alone will stand. In fact, it will one day triumph, for its teachings take hold of men's minds more and more each day." Origen was martyred after torture and imprisonment.

Here is what some of the other early church leaders had to say about the persecutions.

> If any ruler whatever prohibits the Greek philosophy, that philosophy vanishes immediately. But our doctrine on its very first proclamation was prohibited by both kings and tyrants, as well as by local rulers and governors. In fact, they tried

as far as they could to exterminate it. However, it flourishes the more. For it does not die as do human doctrine! Rather, it remains unchecked, although prophesied as destined to be persecuted to the end.

—Clement of Alexandria

Tertullian had much to say about the persecutions:

Although torn and bleeding under your tortures, we cry out, "We worship God through Christ." With our hands thus stretched out and up to God, rend us with your iron claws, hang us up on crosses, wrap us in flames, take our heads from us with the sword, let loose the wild beasts on us. The very attitude of a Christian praying is one of preparation for all punishment.

If a Christian is pointed at, he glories in it. If dragged to trial, he does not resist. If accused, he makes no defense. When questioned, he confesses. When condemned, he rejoices.

We are regarded as persons to be hated by all men for the sake of the Name, just as it was written. And we are delivered up by our nearest of kin, also as it was written. We are brought before magistrates, examined, tortured, make confession [of Christ], and are ruthlessly killed, as it was written.

Hippolytus spoke of betrayal: "For the church is afflicted and pressed, not only by the Jews, but also by the Gentiles. It is also afflicted by those who are called Christians, but are not such in reality." Because of his works, Hippolytus was exiled to Sardinia to be force worked in the mines where he died from inhumane working conditions.

ROBERT COOK

Cyprian was born around A.D. 200 to wealthy pagan parents; he taught rhetoric and literature and was a magician who practiced black magic, using demons to attack his adversaries. His name is derived from the worship of Aphrodite on the island of Cyprus. He converted in about A.D. 246. After his conversion, he became renowned for his spiritually miraculous gifts and became deacon, priest, and bishop where he became known as "Cyprian of Carthage." During the persecution of Emperor Diocletian, Cyprian went into hiding and covertly ministered to his flock, for which he was condemned as a coward, but if it had been his time to be caught, it would have happened. Later, after the persecution subsided, the question arose of whether or not a brother in Christ who had caved in under the persecution and denied their faith in Christ or gave up their brethren to be persecuted could be readmitted to the Church. There were many who believed that these apostates should not be accepted back into the church, but Cornelius, who was pope at the time, disagreed. Cyprians beliefs were aligned with Cornelius's, and his vigorous defense of Cornelius's call for strictness under stringent conditions but ultimate forgiveness for the truly contrite heart helped to avert a dangerous schism in the church. Cyprian was later seized and taken to Damascus where he was tortured; because of his faith, he never wavered. He was brought back to Carthage and was beheaded. He felt this way about the persecution:

> The Lord has desired his family to be tested. Because a long peace had corrupted the discipline that had been divinely delivered to us, the heavenly rebuke has aroused our faith. For our faith was slipping and slumbering. Although we

deserved more for our sins, yet the most merciful Lord has so moderated all things that all that has happened has seemed more like a trial then a persecution.

In America, we have had peace for a long time. We have a whole generation who has never seen hard times, and the church has been corrupted due to false doctrinal teaching on a number of subjects and the tolerance of that which should never have been tolerated within our ranks.

The Holy Spirit teaches and shows us that the army of the devil is not to be feared. And if the foe should declare war against us, our hope consists in that very war itself. In Exodus 1:12 (KJV), the Bible declares that we the people of God are actually multiplied and increased by afflictions.

Lactantius spoke these pieces of wisdom:

> "Our persecutors act with a blind and unreasonable fury, which we see but they do not. For it is not the men themselves who persecute us for they have no cause of anger against the innocent. Rather it is those defiled and abandoned spirits (demonic spirits) by whom the truth is both known and hated. Those spirits infiltrate their minds and goad them to fury in their ignorance. For as long as there is peace among the people of God, these spirits flee from the righteous and fear them.
> There for whatever things wicked rulers plan against us, God Himself permits to be done. And yet these most unjust persecutors to whom the name of God is subject of reproach and mockery must not think that they will escape with impunity.

ROBERT COOK

In Revelation 2:13, Jesus says, "I know your works and where you dwell, even where Satan's seat is: and you hold fast my name, and have not denied my faith, even in those days wherein Antipas was my faithful martyr, who was slain among you, where Satan dwells" (KJV). This is the only time that the man Antipas is spoken of in the Bible, but secularly, there is a historical record of Antipas and his involvement with the church. Antipas, whose name means *against all* was the bishop of Pergamos in A.D. 83. According to tradition, Antipas was consecrated by the Apostle John. The people who were living in Pergamos were worshipping demons who had appeared to them, but because of Antipas, the evil spirits told their worshipers that they could no longer dwell among them or accept their sacrifices because of the power of Christ through Antipas that was casting them out. Antipas was also known for the gift of healing especially those that had severely afflicted teeth.

Antipas fought against the institution of the Nicolation system (which God hates) of the separation of the priests and laity. Throughout their history they gave heed to seducing spirits and the doctrines of demons. Antipas was captured by the idolaters of Pergamos and brought to the governor of Pergamos, who tried to convince Antipas that the older things were more honorable than the new. Antipas was steadfast in his beliefs, and after refusing to pinch some incense to throw into the red-hot, copper, bull-shaped altar of Caesar, he was thrown into the bull where he prayed fervently, glorifying the great power of God and thanking him for being worthy to suffer for his love while roasting to death. Is that radical or not? Although nothing more is spoken about Antipas in the Bible, it is no wonder that he received an honorable mention in the Bible from Jesus. Contrary to common beliefs, Jesus considers it an honorable act of faith to die in his name. Further proof of that is the martyrdom of Stephen, who was the first to die in the name of Christ. Every place where Jesus is spoken of in heaven, he is always sitting at the right hand of God, except in Acts chapter 7, verses 55 and 56. Some of the members of the local synagogue had begun to dispute with Stephen, and he was answering their questions with the truth, which made them very angry with him, so they went to him and began to bite on his flesh with their teeth. At the moment they were doing this, Stephen looked up to heaven and saw Jesus standing at the right hand of God, and when Stephen told his persecutors what he had seen, they became even more enraged and stoned him to death. The point here is that Jesus was giving Stephen a standing ovation, honoring Stephen for giving his only life for his Lord and Savior.

ROBERT COOK

Pagan Ritual Is Adopted into the Church:
How Could This Have Happened?

All and all, the single most common reason for persecuting the early church was because they refused to participate in pagan worship, pagan rituals, pagan holidays, or even the smallest of acts, such as pinching a small bit of incense and casting it into a fire in the name of the emperor of Rome, who was just a man-made deity by other men. These early Christians died because they wouldn't become corrupted or allow their church to become corrupted, and their martyred numbers could have reached into many millions given the fact that these persecutions lasted for about 230 years. For whatever reason, the Jerusalem church faded out and the seat of the church was switched over to Rome and all of the efforts of the early church leaders to keep paganism out of the church were for nothing. Man has a real bad habit of messing up what God has given man to take care of.

Not long after the church and state became one and Christianity was declared the official religion of the Roman Empire around A.D. 313, the church leaders in Rome began to compromise the integrity of the church.

As we have already read, there were certain traditions that the Romans had and some of these traditions were carried over into the new theocratic state from the pagan empire, which opened the door to bring into the church many nonbiblical traditions and holidays, and nearly all of them are pagan in origin. The church leaders, while trying to create a church that was universally more attractive to the world, began to make compromises in that they began to allow pagan holidays and rituals to be accepted and practiced as part of the worship of God and his Son. A government mandate that bled over from the Roman Empire was that everybody who was part of the Roman Empire must become a Christian. So instead of the pagan government trying to force the Christians to partake in pagan worship and ritual, it was the Christian government trying to force the pagan masses to convert over to Christianity, which was the reasoning behind the compromises. So a multitude of nonbiblical pagan traditions and practices were grafted into Christianity.

In the first three hundred years of the church, the only holidays and practices that were sanctioned by the Word of God were the traditions and rituals that Jesus practiced or commanded or were adopted from Judaism. The early church did commemorate the death and resurrection of Christ but it was nothing even close to what we do today and it was done during the Passover celebration.

According to the Bible, the Last Supper of Christ took place on the day of the feast of the Passover, which is the fourteenth day of the first month Nisan of the Jewish calendar, which is our month of April, and it was on this same day that Jesus was betrayed by Judas and crucified on the cross (the Jewish day starts and ends at the setting of the sun, and it was after the sunset) This day also represents the day the sacrificial lamb was killed and its blood used to save the Israelite people from the angel of death just before they exited Egypt (Exodus 12:6). Though Easter Sunday lands on different dates, those dates are always after the fourteenth of Nisan. Even at the time of Polycarp there was a deep division in the church between the Jerusalem church and the Roman church as to when the Passover should be commemorated. The tradition of celebrating the Passover (according to Polycarp) was to be done on the fourteenth of April, which was in line with the apostolic teachings of both of the Apostles John the Revelator and Paul of Tarshish, and it was three days later on the seventeenth of April that Christ was raised from the grave just before the sunrise. This would mean that the day the church would celebrate the resurrection of Christ would take place on a different day of the week each year because the day of the Passover feast migrates backwards on our Gregorian calendar for three years and then is propelled forward twenty-nine days because the Jewish year has fewer days in a year then we do. In 1992, for example the fourteenth of Nisan fell on April 17. In 1994, the fourteenth of Nisan fell on March 26. In the year 2005, the fourteenth of Nisan fell on April 10. In the year 2007, it fell on March 20, and in the year 2009, it fell once again on March 26.

But the Roman church wanted the celebration to fall on the same day every year, and they wanted it to be what they understood to be the first day of the week, so they changed the celebration to Sunday, the sixteenth day of April. But the Jerusalem Church continued to calibrate the resurrection of Christ according to the apostolic teachings until sometime in the fourth century. If it was an apostolic teaching, then even today we should be celebrating the resurrection of Christ just as the apostles did, which would be according to the Jewish calendar, and indeed the Orthodox Christians still do. When the Roman church instituted the change, many of the early Jerusalem church leaders were very upset that the Roman church would disregard the apostolic teachings so easily with little regard for the consequences of an act of what God considers rebellion against that which he has already decreed.

Anatolius of Laodicea in Syria was one of the frontline scholars of his day in the field of physical sciences and Aristotelian philosophy. He wrote ten books on arithmetic and a treatise on the proper time of the Passover or Paschal celebration and wholly disagreed with the date change. Though the controversy of the date change had been going on for a very long time the date was not officially changed until the Council of Nicaea that was presided over by Emperor/Pope Constantine that changed the date of the resurrection of Christ from a true date to a false date, which some would say is a minor problem. But in the eyes of God, it is a sin like any other sin because God commemorates dates for his reasons, and we have no right to change that which God has designated. God orchestrated the death of his son so that it would fall on the Passover holy day because his son was the sacrificial Lamb, and he sure enough didn't do that so we could change that date over to a pagan date set aside to practice paganism. The Jews believed that as long as the number of daylight hours were longer than the dark hours of the night, the celebration of the Pasch could take place, but if the daylight hours and the dark hours of the night were even or the hours of darkness were more than the hours of daylight, the Pasch/Easter was not to be celebrated. For this reason, Anatolius wrote his treatise on the Pasch, which is the Hebrew Easter.

To us, however with whom it is impossible for all these things to come aptly at one and the same time, namely, the moon's fourteenth, and the Lord's day, and the passing of the equinox, and whom the obligation of the Lord's resurrection binds [us] to keep the Paschal festival on the Lord's day, it is granted that we may extend the beginning of our celebration even to the moon's twentieth. For although the moon of the twentieth does not fill the whole night, yet, rising as it does in the second watch, it illuminates the greater part of the night. Certainly if the rising of the moon should be delayed onto the end of two watches, that is to say, to midnight, the light would not then exceed the darkness, but the darkness the light. (You see, the Paschal was all about the saving Light of God and not the darkness of Satan. The length of darkness and light were symbolic to the Jew.) But it is clear that in the Paschal feast it is not possible that any part of the darkness should surpass the light; for the festival of the Lord's resurrection is one of light, and there is no fellowship between light and darkness. And if the moon should rise in the third watch, it is clear that the twenty-second or twenty-third of the moon (month) would then be reached, in which it is not possible that there can be a true celebration of the resurrection. For those who determine that the festival may be kept at this age of the moon, are not only unable to make that good by authority of Scripture, but turn into the crime of sacrilege and contumacy, (which means "stubborn resistance to authority") and incur the peril of their souls; inasmuch as they affirm that the true light may be celebrated along with something of that power of darkness dominates all.

It is believed that Anatolius of Laodicea was murdered in A.D. 283 by the heretics he spoke out against within the Roman church.

Another early church leader who was against the date change of Easter/Pasch was against it because it was not according to scriptural or apostolic teaching. His name was Polycrates, who was the bishop of Ephesus. He lived from A.D. 130 to 169 and came from a family of church leaders. Not much else is known about him other than his writings and what he believed. He fallowed the teachings of the Apostle John, and he was faithful to the teachings of the gospel. He stood on the belief that the teachings of the Bible were above those of the accepted pagan traditions of Rome. He was a spokesperson for the churches in Asia Minor and refused to accept the authority of the bishop of Rome or Roman tradition. He claimed that his life would be governed by Jesus and not the opinions of men. Here is what he recorded on the date change:

As for us, then, we scrupulously observe the exact day, neither adding nor taking away. For in Asia great luminaries have gone to their rest who will rise again on the day of the coming of the Lord. These all kept Easter on the fourteenth day, in accordance with the Gospel. Seven of my relatives were bishops, and I am the eighth, and my relatives always observed the day when the people put away the leaven.

ROBERT COOK

The fact of the matter is that if we are to celebrate the Lord's sacrificial death on the fourteenth of April, which is the first day of the Pasch, and the day that the Passover feast is to be eaten, then the emphasis was not so much on resurrection as it was on the sacrifice of Jesus; however, in keeping with the Passover/Paschal celebration, we would still celebrate the resurrection of Christ on the third day after the Passover feast, which would be the Day of the First Fruits, according to Jewish tradition. And Jesus was the first fruits for a new beginning with a new theme and a new opportunity for us to be saved from ourselves. He willingly gave up his life and subjected himself to be tortured so that we might be saved from eternal death. Praise God Almighty!

> "Now that we know how the early church leaders in Jerusalem felt about the Passover, what does the Bible say about it? In 1 Corinthians 5:7, 8, Paul says, "Purge out therefore the old leaven that you may be a new lump, as you are unleavened. For even Christ our Passover is sacrificed for us. Therefore let us keep the feast, not with old leaven, neither with the leaven of the malice and wickedness; but with the unleavened bread of sincerity and truth" (KJV).

By these two verses, we know that Christ is our sacrificial Passover Lamb whose blood has saved us from eternal death, and Paul is instructing the church at Corinth to observe and keep the Passover just as it was laid out by God in the Old Testament. How is it that we are supposed to take scripture at its word but choose to do the exact opposite of what Paul and God

THE JERUSALEM CHURCH

have instructing us to do is beyond me. This is how we are instructed in the Old Testament.

> These are the feasts of the Lord, even holy convocations, which you shall proclaim in their seasons. In the fourteenth day of the first month at even is the Lord's Passover.
>
> Leviticus 23:4, 5, KJV

> Take heed to yourselves that you be not snared by following them (the heathen gods), after that they be destroyed from before you; and that you enquire not after their gods, saying, "How did these nations serve their gods? Even so will I do likewise?" You shall not do so to the Lord your God; for every abomination to the Lord which he hates, have they done to their gods; for even their sons and their daughters they have burnt in the fire to their gods. What thing so ever I command you observe to do it; you shall not add to nor diminish from it.
>
> Deuteronomy 12:30–32, KJV

God was and is always in complete control, and he didn't allow his son to be sacrificed on the same day as the Passover feast nor did he raise Jesus from the grave during the Passover celebration because he simply felt like it. To God, those events were most important and very dear to his heart.

There were many church leaders in Asia Minor besides Polycrates who were contrary to and refused to accept the authority of any Roman bishop when it was in conflict with biblical teachings.

Sun worship and celebrations related to sun worship

ROBERT COOK

were the most popular before and after Christianity came along, so in order to seduce the pagans who refused to completely abandon their ceremonies, festivals, and holidays, the Roman church leaders decided to adopt into the Christian holidays pagan rituals and celebrations by changing their names, reasons for their celebrations, and practices, linking them with Christian events, as well as with Christian personalities, and the celebration of Easter was no exception.

Long before the birth of Christ, there were people who worshiped the sun, and this religion dates back all the way to the tower of Babel. The name of this sun god was Tammuz, who, in the Old Testament, is known as Baal, Baalim, Bel, Molech, and later known in the Roman world as Mithras. He was a man-made deity by other men. He was according to legend the illegitimate son of Semiramis, who was the wife of Nimrod. For six thousand years, she has been referred to as the queen of heaven and the mother of God. She is mentioned as the queen of heaven four times in the book of Jeremiah. In Greece, she was also known as Aphrodite, Artemis, Athena, and so on. In the Roman Empire, she was otherwise known as Venus, Diana, Juno, Terra, and to the Israelites she was known as Ashtaroth. (Judges 2:13; 1 Kings 11:5 and 33; 2 Kings 23:13, KJV). Semiramis became the goddess of the sun, the moon, fertility, and the giver of life; she claimed that her son Tammuz was Nimrod reborn and the promised seed, i.e., the savior. The fact that Semiramis claimed her son to be the savior shows that she knew something about the prophecies of God. At the very least, she knew that the Son of God was coming to save the world from itself. Legend has it that after Tammuz was killed by a wild boar, he descended into the underworld. But Semiramis wept over her son for forty days (Lent), after which he was resurrected and each year thereafter a spring festival was held to commemorate his resurrection. She is also known as the "mother goddess," with names like Ishtar, Astarte, Eastre, and Ostera, and as Mother Nature, she was worshiped as the goddess of spring, sexuality, and birth.

As the Roman church began to separate itself from its Hebrew roots, it began to adopt into the worship of God more and more pagan practices, and after Constantine, who was a sun worshiper before he converted to Christianity, made himself emperor/pope, the paganization of the church accelerated. Almost overnight, pagan temples became churches, and pagan parishioners and priests became Christians. This is where we get the name for our first day of the week, Sunday, and how it came to be that on Easter Sunday we will go to church early for a sunrise service, literally watching the sunrise, which is supposed to be symbolic of the rise of Christ, but is still a pagan ritual. The problem with this sunrise service to commemorate the raising of Jesus from the dead is that Jesus didn't rise with the rising sun; he was already raised while it was still dark just before dawn. In Matthew 28:1-6 (KJV), the Bible doesn't say anything about Jesus coming out of the tomb at the time of the rising sun because even before the angle was sitting on the stone, Christ had already risen from the dead and had already left the tomb, which means the tomb was empty before sunrise. How is it that we can be so convinced that having a sun rise service is right in the eyes of God when it is wrong according to his word?

ROBERT COOK

Easter:
What Is It?

As time went on, the rift between the Roman church and the Jerusalem church continued to widen until the Roman church started excommunicating those who would not abide by the date and pagan ritual set forth by the Roman church and all resistance was gone and every voice of dissention was silenced. According to the Roman church, the tradition of observing the forty days of Lent is for soul searching, repentance, reflection, taking stock of one's life, a time of fasting and prayer in preparation for the Easter celebration when the faithful rededicate themselves and new converts are instructed in the faith and prepared for baptism. It is taught that Lent is an apostolic commandment, and by observing the forty days of Lent, one imitates Jesus' time in the wilderness after his baptism. All of this sounds really good but these are not apostolic commandments. They are however pagan rituals. First of all, we must remember that all of the apostles and early church leaders were all gone by the middle of the fourth century (A.D. 350), and there is not one piece of documentation, both secularly and religiously, written by any of the apostles commanding us to observe the forty days of Lent. Not only that but also in the book of Ezekiel, chapter eight, there is proof that the forty days of Lent are pagan and God hates it. Verses 14–17:

> Then He brought me to the door of the gate of the Lord's house which was toward the north; and, behold, there sat women weeping for Tammuz. Then said He to me, "Have you seen this, O son of man?" And He brought me into the inner court of the Lord's house, and behold, at the door of the temple of the Lord, between the porch and altar, were about five and twenty men, with their back toward the temple of the Lord, and their faces toward the east; and they were worshipping the sun toward the east. Then He said to me, "Have you seen this, O son of man? Is it a light thing to the house of Judah that they commit the abominations which they commit here? For they have filled the land with violence, and have returned to provoke me to anger: and lo, they put the branch to their nose."

As you can see from these verses above, God hates these pagan rituals with a passion and the idea that Lent is an apostolic commandment is a lie. If Lent were truly an apostolic commandment, there would be scripture to reinforce the idea. The forty days of Lent would be biblically sanctioned, and there would be no question as to whether or not it was of God. But since the forty days of Lent are not spoken of anywhere in the Bible, this tells us that the whole concept of the forty days of Lent are a man-made ritual with its origins steeped in paganism. Since the sun rises in the east, these verses are the first documented proof that the season of Lent and the sunrise service existed long before 484 BC when this prophecy was given.

ROBERT COOK

The word *Easter* appears in the Bible only once in Acts 12:4 (KJV), but here the word is used to speak of the Passover feast.

Otherwise, the name *Easter* is a heathen term derived from a goddess named Eostra by the Anglo Saxons and Ostara by the Germanic peoples, and her name means "movements toward the rising sun."

Most everything else that is practiced or considered tradition on Easter comes from paganism. Hot cross buns were used as ritual bread served at the spring feast of Eostra and the cross represents the solar wheel, which represents pagan cosmology, the study of the evolution of the universe. Missionaries from Rome tried to convince the pagans not to practice the ritual but were unsuccessful, so they gave up on trying to stop the pagan ritual, compromised the word of God and adopted the ritual into the church by blessing the buns.

In ancient paganism, the rabbit wasn't a rabbit at all; it was a hare. In about the second century in Europe, the dominant spring festival was a Saxon celebration in honor of the Saxon goddess Ostara [Eostra], whose sacred animal was the hare. The hare was a symbol of fertility, renewal, and the arrival of spring. Each year at these festivals, hares where sacrificed to Ostara.

The egg is an ancient symbol of rebirth, new life, creation, fertility, and abundance, which figured into many of the festivals. The egg also has played an important role in the ancient mythical accounts of the creation of the world. It was believed that heaven and earth were formed from the two halves (the yoke and the white) of a mysterious world egg. The ancients, long before Christ, regarded the eggs as symbols of the continuing life and resurrection. The Persians and Greeks exchanged them at spring festivals when nature was revived after dying during the winter. Another ancient belief is that a mysterious egg fell from the sky into the Euphrates River, and the fish in the river rolled the egg to the shore and man was created or hatched from that egg. This is where we get the tradition of egg rolling every year at the White House. During the reign of Constantine, the symbolism of the egg was changed to represent the resurrection of Christ. The eggs would be blessed, after which, they would be considered holy, which enabled Christians to eat them and present them as gifts during Easter. The date we celebrate Easter changes from year to year because Easter is celebrated the first Sunday after the vernal equinox full moon, which signifies the astronomical arrival of spring and is considered the time to celebrate the rebirth and renewal as nature resurrects itself from the death it suffered from winter. Even this practice is pagan because it doesn't take into account the command to celebrate the Passover as the apostolic teaching commands us to do.

ROBERT COOK

The Eucharist:

Is It Truly a Holy Thing of God?

As we have discussed before, Semiramis, who is otherwise known as the mother of God and the queen of heaven who bore Tammuz who also claimed that she conceived via immaculate conception. The result was the beginning of the mother-child worship. Centuries later, Egyptian priests developed a ritual known as the transubstantiation, which was meant to pull out of a portion of the spirit of Ra, the Egyptian sun god in order to put that portion of spirit into a wafer, after which they would eat their wafer for spiritual nourishment.

At this point, I would like to make a declaration. The Eucharist is among many inanimate (lifeless) objects used in the worship of God and his Son. They are declared to be holy, but the word *holy* in any biblical dictionary means "one who lives without sin. When speaking of God the word "holy" means sinless or without sin." Since these ritual objects are in fact lifeless and do not live, it is impossible for them to commit sin and therefore impossible for them to live without sin. So to call something that is lifeless that is fashioned with the hands of men, as if it were equal to God, is to commit blaspheme, which is a sin against the person of God.

Ancient peoples like the Brahmins who were

ancient Hindu educators, scholars, and preachers in Hinduism, taught that rice cakes that were sacrificed to the gods were substitutes for the real flesh and blood of humans, which were then converted into real flesh and blood by the works of the priests. In other cultures and primitive tribes, ceremonies existed in which pagan worshipers eat images of their god that was made from grain flour that was kneaded, using human blood to make the dough, after which a priest would turn into a god using a magical formula.

Even the Aztecs as well believed in the ceremonial transformation of consecrated bread into the actual flesh and blood of various gods.

The pagan belief was that the god could be called down from heaven to change that which is to be sacrificed from nothing into the flesh and blood of their god, and so this was the concept that the Roman church adopted, which is known as the transubstantiation by which Christ is called down from heaven and changes the wafer and wine into the real flesh and blood of Christ after it is consumed.

In Matthew 26:26–28, Christ took the bread and blessed it before he gave it to his disciples to eat; then he gave thanks to God for the wine. As we can read from the Scriptures, Jesus was very much alive and not bleeding from any wounds when he instituted the practice of taking the communion. By these facts, we know that the bread and wine were purely symbolic and were never intended to be considered the real flesh and blood of Christ. While it is true that partaking of the communion when one is ill-prepared spiritually can make the partaker sick, it is the condition of the heart that Jesus is concerned with and not the flesh.

ROBERT COOK

In reality, the Eucharist and all it represents is pagan, but the institution of the communion, which was blessed by Christ as it was written in the word of God, is blessed.

St. Valentine's Day:
Where Did It Come From

Lupercalia was a festival that was celebrated in ancient times in honor of a deity, the name of which is not certain. No one knows for sure what the function of this deity was. It could have been the protector of flocks against wolves, the god of agriculture and shepherds, or it could have been Rumina, the goddess whose temple stood near the fig tree under which the she-wolf suckled Romulus and Remus.

The legend begins with the grandfather of Romulus and Remus, who was king of the ancient Italian city of Alba Longa. Numitor was ousted by his brother Amulius, who made Numitor's daughter, Rhea Silva, a vestal virgin and was forbidden to marry because her children would be the rightful heirs to the throne. Then Mars, the god of war, fell in love with her, and she gave birth to twin sons. Fearing that the two boys would grow up to claim the throne, Amulius had them placed in a basket and thrown into the freezing flood waters of the Tiber River. When the waters receded, the basket settled on the shore of Palantine Hill, where they were discovered by a she-wolf who suckled and nurtured them.

The boys were later found by a man named Faustulus,

who was the king's shepherd. He took them home, and he and his wife adopted and named them. They grew up to be bold and strong young men who eventually led a revolt against Amulius, killing him and restoring the kingdom back to their bloodline. Later, the two young men decided to found a small city on the spot where the she-wolf had nursed them. While building the city, Romulus killed his brother for making fun of the walls he was building and continued to build the new city, naming it Roma after himself, which today is the city of Rome.

Since the month of February occurred later in the year in the ancient Roman calendar than it does today, the festival of Lupercalia was held in the Lupercal cave in early spring and was regarded as a festival of purification and fertility. During the festival, vestal virgins would bring cakes made from the first fruits of the previous year's harvest of grain to a certain fig tree where two naked young men would assist the vestal virgins in the sacrifice of a dog and a goat. The blood of the sacrifice would then be smeared on the foreheads of the two young men and wiped away with wool dipped in milk. This and other practices at the festival were said to provide purification from curses, bad luck, and infertility.

Soon the Palantine Hill became the powerful city of the Roman Empire, and there is no doubt that the festival of Lupercalia's importance in the Roman dogma because records show that Mark Antony, who was master of the college of priests, chose the date of the festival, which was the fourteenth of February, as the proper time to offer the crown to Julius Caesar. Wherever the Roman armies went, they carried with them the customs of Lupercalia, and among their conquests were France and Britain. One of these customs was what was known as the lover's lottery, where names of the available maidens were placed in a box and eligible young men would draw out a name and would then accept the girl whose name he drew as his love for the duration of the festival and sometimes longer.

In the late fifth century, the Roman church under Pope Gelasius I, in its efforts to dismantle the pagan pantheons, decided to come up with its own lottery and festival. So in the year A.D. 496, Pope Gelasius did away with the festival of Lupercalia, declaring it to be pagan and immoral. He chose Valentine as the patron saint of lovers, who would be honored at the new festival on the fourteenth of February every year. In the lottery, one would pull the name of a saint out of a box and would study and try to emulate that saint. In this way, the church compromised its integrity by sanctioning a pagan celebration it could not suppress. They called that which was not of God as if it were. There is, however, some considerable confusion as to which Saint Valentine the pope was referring to since there were three Saint Valentines who were listed in the early martyrs under the date of February 14. One was a Roman priest who continued to marry couples in secret after the Emperor Claudius had cancelled all marriages because he wanted more men to join the military, another was a Bishop of Interamna, Italy, which is now called Terni, and another is said to have lived and died in Africa, of which there is little known.

There was also a belief during the Middle Ages in Europe that birds chose their mates during the middle of February. So consequently, February 14 was dedicated to love, and Europeans observed it by writing love letters and sending small gifts to their lovers. According to legend, the first Valentine cards were created by a young French Duke of Orleans named Charles who was captured in battle and held in the Tower of London who was a prolific psalmist and wrote countless poems to his wife. About sixty of his love letters still remain among the royal papers in the British Museum.

By the late 1700s, Valentine cards were being produced by printers but became racy and sexually suggestive, causing several countries, including America, to ban the practice of exchanging cards. In the 1870s, the first American publisher of Valentine cards was a printer and artist named Esther Howland. Her cards were elaborately laced and cost five to ten dollars apiece. Although the technology to extract cocoa from the cocoa bean was used by 1528, it was not made edible until 1847. Some twenty years later, the Cadbury brothers discovered how to make chocolate even smoother and sweeter, and by 1868, the Cadburys turned out their first box of chocolate and their first heart-shaped Valentine's Day box of chocolate candy was produced during the year 1870

Today, thanks to the enormous level of Roman paganism that still exists, we now celebrate a St. Valentine's Day that is steeped in pagan gods, beliefs, and ritual that has nothing at all in common with the gospel of Christ. The single most common symbol besides the heart is Cupid, who is the son of Venus, who was the Roman goddess of love and beauty. In ancient Greece, Cupid is known as Amor or Eros, the son of Aphrodite. The Greeks believed that Eros was the god of love and the force behind all creation. Eros is where we get the English word *erotica* from, and Aphrodite is where we get the English word *aphrodisiac*. In ancient times, Cupid was portrayed as a young, handsome, Adonis

ROBERT COOK

like, mythological man, but somehow his appearance has been changed into an innocent, cubby, and playful little cherub who shoots his little arrows into the hearts of unsuspecting men and women, causing love-sickness, heartaches, and the unsuspecting recipient of the heart-piercing arrows to fall in love with the first member of the opposite sex he or she lays eyes on. One can color a pagan god any which way one wants to, but it is still a pagan god.

As I mentioned before, ancient Europeans believed that birds mated in the middle of February, and there are some that actually do. Birds like the Missel Thrush, the Partridge, and the Blackbird really do mate in the middle of February, which is the reason lovebirds became connected with St. Valentine's Day, and the most favorite of the lovebirds is the dove that is always bearing a message alone or in a pair. In Greek mythology, the dove was sacred to Venus and other deities of love. Even in the word of God, the dove delivered a massage to Noah and in the Song of Solomon, he sings about the sound of the turtledove in the spring. In many lands in both ancient and modern times, the dove is seen as magical and to have been used to divine the future and let us not forget that it was the Holy Spirit that descended down from heaven onto Jesus in the form of a dove.

The goal in all of this is to inform the family of God that what they think of as something innocent and not harmful to the soul is in fact a deceptively disguised form of pagan ritual that God hates.

The Birth of Jesus:
Exactly When Was He Born?

We cannot know for sure the exact day on which Christ was born because the Bible is not precise about his birth date. But using the Word of God, we can know the time of year he was born in. A normal year on the Hebrew calendar consists of twelve lunar months of twenty-nine or thirty days for a total of 354 days in a year instead of 365. Twelve out of every nineteen Jewish years needs forty-eight weeks of temple duties to be done and three festival weeks of temple coverage in which priests perform certain tasks and rituals. The family of Zacharias, who was the father of John the Baptist, was among those families of priests that were selected by lot long ago, and there were certain times during the year that he had to be at the temple to officiate. Luke 1:5 says, "There was in the days of Herod, the king of Judea, a certain priest named Zacharias, of the division of Abia: and his wife was of the daughters of Aaron, and her name was Elisabeth" (KJV). Abia or Abijah was a descendant of Aaron, which means he was from the tribe of the Levites. Under Nehemiah, Abia was a leading priest who signed a covenant to obey the laws of God after the Israelites returned from exile in Babylon, and it is from his house of priests that Zechariah is a descendant. Luke 1:8–9 says that Zacharias was serving as priest before God "according to the custom of the priesthood, his lot fell to burn incense when he went into the temple of the Lord." So it was after Zacharias had served his time in the temple that he went home, and shortly after, his wife Elizabeth conceived.

There were twenty-four courses of priests who served in the temple, and each course served at different times during the year, one week at a time, and all twenty-four courses served in the temple during the three festival weeks, which are the Feast of the Tabernacles, the Feast of Unleavened Bread, and the Feast of Weeks. When all of the twenty-four courses had served, they started all over again.

Like us, Judaism has more than one beginning for a new year in one year. We have a school year that starts in the months of August or September, depending on where you live. There are many businesses that have a fiscal year that starts at various times of the year, and our calendar a new year starts on January 1. In Judaism, there is a new year that starts in August for the tithing of animals, and there is another new year that starts in March or April for counting the reign of kings, giving of the first fruits and eating the Feast of Unleavened Bread and a new year for the start of a sabbatical or jubilee years, which begin at this time and also commemorate the anniversary of Creation. It is believed that on this day, God opens the Lamb's Book of Life, observes his creatures, and decides their fate for the coming year. And still another new year that starts in the last half of January or the first half of February, which is for determining when the first fruits from trees can be harvested and eaten. But the new year we are

ROBERT COOK

concerned about is the Feast of Unleavened Bread. The time of the year when the priests began their temple service can be calculated using scripture. We know that the first designated holiday is the Passover and the second holiday is the Feast of Unleavened Bread (Exodus 13:1–15, KJV), and it is that time of year in the month of Abib/March and April that God required the Israelites to sanctify to him all of the firstborn, both man and beast, which are the first fruits. The month of Abib is also called Nisan, and the word means "green ears of grain," and according to Exodus 12:1–20, it is the first month of the year: "This month shall be to you the beginning of months: it shall be the first month of the year to you" (KJV). On the fourteenth day of this month is the first Sabbath, and the twenty-first day is the second Sabbath, and we know this because there are no other Sabbaths spoken of before these two, so by this we know when the Sabbaths began.

The name of this month speaks of green ears of grain, along with the firstborn. In Leviticus 23:5–16, we find in verses 10–14 the first fruits of the fields are brought and offered to the Lord on the same day as the flesh. These verses have told us that the priestly courses started in the month of Abib/Nisan, which is the last part of March or the first part of April for us. Among the required rituals done during the Feast of Unleavened Bread is the waving of the sheaf on the first day after the first Sabbath. (Leviticus 23:10–12, KJV), And we know from the meaning of the name of that month and from verse 14 that at this time the grain in the fields are still green. It is a time to begin the spring harvest and earring or re-plowing the fields for the summer crop.

Seven Sabbaths or fifty days (Leviticus 23:15–22)

from the day after the Sabbath and the beginning of the Feast of Unleavened Bread brings us to the Feast of Weeks, which is otherwise known as the Pentecost, the Feast of Harvest, and the Feast of First Fruits, but for the sake of argument, we will call it the day of Pentecost, and it is celebrated at the end of the spring harvest.

We know from 1 Chronicles 24:10 that the descendants of Abijah, who was a grandson of Aaron, were chosen to serve in the temple by the Urim and the Thummim, which means "lights and perfection" (Exodus 28:30, KJV). According to the Jewish historian Josephus, they were two pieces of precious stones that were put into a bag and one or the other or both would glow, which was one of the ways God would communicate his judgments to the priests, and only a priest could look into the bag.

So it was that the house of Abijah was to serve in the temple during the eighth week and the ninth week of the year because the ninth week was one of the three celebrations when the people or a representatives of all Jewish families were to come to the temple in Jerusalem to give offerings, to pray, and to worship the Lord God Almighty. This means that Zacharias's service in the temple for a feast took place in the last half of May or the first half of June. In Luke 1:23, 24, the Bible says that after Zacharias had served in the temple for his allotted time, he left and went home; then verse 24 says, "And after those days (his days of service) his wife Elisabeth conceived, and hid herself five months." So by these verses, we know that Elisabeth conceived sometime during the month of June or the first half of July, as the word *after* is speaking specifically of the period of time directly after Zacharias returned from the temple in Jerusalem. We know from scripture that Jesus was conceived six months after the conception of John the Baptist: "And, behold, your cousin Elisabeth, she has also conceived a son in her old age: and this is the sixth month with her, who was called barren" (Luke 32:36, KJV). This verse tells us that John the Baptist was conceived six months before Jesus was, so if we move up three more months, we come to the Pesach/ Passover festival and the birth of John the Baptist, which took place either in the last half of the month of March or within the first half or middle of April. Now, if we believe that the birth of John took place in the first half or the middle of April, it would mean that Jesus (who was born six months later) was born in the last half of September, which would be during the Feast of the Tabernacles, which is the last of the three events that required a pilgrimage to Jerusalem to worship God Almighty in his temple and to give sacrifices and offerings to the Lord. The Feast of Tabernacles is Israel's Thanksgiving feast in which they acknowledge God's provision for them, and there is no doubt at all that Jesus Christ is God's provision for us, which is still providing for us a way out of eternal damnation and darkness. Glory be to the giver of life eternal.

Christmas:
Is It Really Biblical

Christmas is the single biggest holiday of the year, and it is considered to be one hundred percent Christian. Unfortunately, it is not at all biblical, nor is it sanctioned by God or his Son, Jesus, whose birth is the reason for the season, or so we have been taught to believe. And when the subject is brought up about whether or not Christmas is of God or not, most Christians become very angry when they are told that the Word of God itself speaks out against decorating trees because it is a form of pagan worship and ritual. In fact, just as it was in the early church, believers are so hung up on their holidays that they refuse to give them up, no matter what the Word of God says. One season, there was a full-page advertisement in the local newspaper from Liberty Collage and Liberty Counsel offering to defend in court for free anybody who was persecuted because of Christmas by the law or forced to remove or take down a nativity scene from their house or school or business. So I fired off an e-mail to them, quoting scripture and asking them, "Why are you defending that which God himself has called a heathen, pagan practice?" Liberty Counsel never sent back a reply, but a professor of theology or something like that sent me a reply asking me, "How many souls have you brought to the Lord this year?" My reply was that I didn't have any idea of how many souls I had brought to the Lord this year. Because I have this big sign on both sides of my van that says "Christ is coming! Be ready when He gets here because if you get Left Behind, there will not be a second chance!" And I have Matthew 25:1–13 as a reference on my sign also. Everywhere I go, all day long, people read my sign, so I don't know how many seeds God has planted via my sign, but God does.

The point is that even when a well-educated professor of theology who works in a well-known theological college is confronted with scripture that, beyond the shadow of a doubt, states that decorating trees is considered by God to be a heathen/pagan practice and God tells us not to do it, he completely bypasses the subject all together and tries to divert the focus of the subject matter to something else and to lay guilt on me in the process. What a joke. He didn't even try to dispute the Scriptures I sent him.

On another occasion, I walked up to the pastor of a Church of God and read from Jeremiah 10:1–5, which tells us not to learn the ways of the heathen (the word *heathen* is used to speak of pagan peoples or nations) and speaks against decorating trees in celebration of anything because that was what pagan nations did in the worship of false gods. He just stood there and looked at me. The expression on his face never changed, and he never said one single word one way or another. At the time that I showed him these Scriptures, there was a twelve-foot Christmas (the word Christmas coming from the two words *Christ Mass,* which was a specific kind of church service that was invented and implemented by the Roman church to celebrate the birth of

ROBERT COOK

Jesus.) tree, and once he received this revelation, his first reaction should have been to take down the decorated tree, but instead he did nothing about it. Of course, if he had taken down the decorated tree and declared it to be a pagan ritual and that God spoke against it, he probably would have lost seventy-five percent, if not all, of his congregation, which I am sure weighed in on his decision to do nothing in spite of what he had just learned about what the Word of God says.

As far back as we know, the tree has been a part of and a tool used by Satan in the temptation and downfall of man. In the book of Genesis, it was the fruit of the tree of life that Satan used to temp Eve into disobeying the very first commandment of God to his creation. Many ancient forms of pagan worship include tree veneration as a major object of nature worship, and even today in many parts of Europe and other areas of the world, it is a custom to cut down a tree and bring it into the village where it is set up with many rejoicings. Ancient philosophers such as Aristotle and Plutarch considered trees to have perceptions, passions, and the ability to reason. Men would put themselves into relationship with a tree by hanging personal items such as hair, trinkets, or clothing on the tree. People believed that one could transfer disease or sickness to a tree by fixing hair, nails, clothing or other objects of the sickly to the tree or they inserted these items by force into a hole in the trunk of a tree or they would split the tree, and the patient would pass between the two sides of the tree, after which the recovery of the tree and that of the sick person are intertwined. Both were supposed to heal at the same time together.

In India, when a patient is tormented by a demon, a ritual is performed with a tree to transfer the demon to the tree where it will dwell in peace as long as the tree is left unharmed. The practice of tree veneration has been found in many cultures both ancient and modern. In Buddhist cultures, the veneration of tree spirits has been an important part of Asian cultures since the time of Gautama Buddha in the fifth century. According to Buddhist legend, the boiled milk rice that Sujata (well-born) offered to Siddhartha just before his spiritual awakening had been prepared as a food offering to the spirit of the Bodhi Tree under which Sujata found, seated at the base of the tree, the bodhisattva Gautama Buddha. In Europe, the culture of tree veneration was prevalent among the early Celtic and Nordic peoples of western and northern Europe. Celtic wizards or magicians, who were otherwise known as Druids, picked out sacred tree groves for their ritual performances. The Celtic peoples also believed that every kind of tree and plant had value and worshiped them for their unique character and properties. Oak trees, for example, were believed to be especially powerful carriers of magic wisdom for those who could tap into the inner essence of the oak tree. The Nordic peoples of Scandinavia believed that any tree that didn't lose its foliage during the bitter cold of the long freezing winters was hosting a tree spirit of everlasting life. Such trees were called evergreens. In Arab countries, the sacred trees are inhabited by the jinn or genies and even demons. Sacrifices of sheep or goats are made to them, and the blood of the sacrifice is sprinkled at the site or onto the sacred tree. It is believed that when the sick and maimed slept under the sacred tree, they would receive a prescription in their dreams. Even in Islamic beliefs there is a tree growing at the top of Paradise called the Sidir Tree. It is believed that this tree is the "Divine

ROBERT COOK

Tree" that was seen by Mohammed the Prophet on one of his night journeys to Paradise. It is said to have very large fruit and leaves the size of elephant ears with four rivers flowing out from under the tree. The Bedouins who roamed the deserts of the Middle East believed that certain shrubs and trees are the abodes of angels and demons. To injure one of these sacred trees or shrubs is considered to be dangerous, and misfortune will overtake he who would do such an outrage.

Worldwide in all of these cultures, the tree was considered to be the "Axis of the World," a living still point or vertical shaft around which the world turns. In Islamic lore, this axis is considered to be the highest stage of sanctity among Muslim saints and refers to the highest degree of sanctity a Muslim can attain. Another name for the world axis is the world tree and represents what is called the vertical ray that radiates life-giving grace from heaven to earth in the form of sunlight. The axis is the point at which the coldest, darkest part of winter is at its end and the life-giving sun has reached the end of its journey to the south and is beginning its ascent to bring life anew. This is celebrated during the winter solstice in late December.

Now that we know for sure that Jesus was not born in the month of December , we should be asking our-selves, "Why are we taught that December 25 is the birth date of Jesus Christ?" As I said before, for the first three hundred years of the church, neither Christmas nor Easter were celebrated because those celebrations were pagan celebrations that included ritual practices performed during those celebrations. They were con-sidered by the first leaders of the church, including Jesus and his handpicked disciples, to be pagan and a sin against God. Even birthdays were considered to be pagan because only the pagans celebrated them. Indeed, in the only two biblically recorded birthday celebrations, a man was murdered as a part of those birthday celebrations.

The last part of December is the darkest time of the year and the time of the winter solstice. In Rome on December 25, a date chosen by Emperor Aurelian in A.D. 274, to celebrate pagan celebrations because he wanted to compress both celebrations into one. One was the celebration of the birth of Mithras, the Iranian sun god named Sun of Righteousness and was a favorite of the Roman soldiers, and the other celebration was the birth of the "unconquered sun," and a few days earlier was the celebration of the winter solstice. Also, by early December, the farmer would have been finished with his autumn planting, which would give way for the grandest pagan festival of the whole year. All of Rome would take part in the celebration of Saturnalia, and it was celebrated between December 17 and December 23 to honor the Roman god named Saturn, who was the god of agriculture. Saturnalia was designated a holy day on which sacrifices and rituals were performed. The temple of Saturn was the oldest temple recorded by the Roman church and had been dedicated during the Saturnalia, when the bonds that fettered the feet of the statue of the pagan god were loosed to symbolize the liberation of the god. After the sacrifice at the temple, there would be a public banquet where the image of the god would be placed in attendance as if he were a guest. The festival was a time when social restrictions were relaxed, public gambling was allowed, less formal dinner clothes were permitted, and slaves were treated as equals. They were permitted to use the dice, wear their masters' clothes, and were waited on at mealtime. During that week, no business was allowed, the serious were barred from the festival, and there was unlimited drinking, games, singing, nakedness, sexual perversions, and other debauchery. It was also a time to visit friends and give gifts.

The Roman church, in seeing that the pagans had so much reverence for these pagan holy days and exalted deities during these celebrations, seized upon the people's reverence for their gods, and the date of December 25 introduced new reason for the season, a new holy day and called it Christ Mass. This is how and when the church compromised its integrity and pagan ritual began to infiltrate into the church and the worship of Christ. The more the church expanded in size and compromises, the more pagan ritual it picked up along the way. Just as the Roman soldiers would bring back to Rome the pagan gods, worship, and rituals from the nations they had conquered, so did the church pick up pagan ritual as it expanded. Every single custom, tradition, and practice that is observed during the Christmas holiday has its origins in paganism, which dates back long before the birth of our Lord and Savior.

The word *mistletoe* for example literally means "dung on a twig," and today it is a tradition to kiss a loved one while standing under a hanging clump of "dung on a twig," and is an intricate part of the Christmas celebrations. Mistletoe can grow by itself, but for the most part, it is a parasitic plant that grows on the trunks or branches of trees. It sends out roots that can penetrate its host tree and sucks life-giving nutrients from the tree. There are two kinds of mistletoe; one is the European mistletoe that has small yellow flowers and white sticky barriers, which are considered poisonous, and grows primarily on apple trees and very rarely on oak trees. The other type of mistletoe is our North American mistletoe, and it grows on mostly oak trees from New Jersey to Florida. Europeans coveted the mistletoe that grew on oak trees, greatly venerated it, and used it as a ceremonial plant, and the Europeans brought their beliefs with them to America in the process of immigration and resettlement. The name of mistletoe was derived from the ancient belief that mistletoe was spread by bird droppings, which was related to the belief that life could spring spontaneously from bird poop. Scientifically speaking, bird droppings are exactly how mistletoe is propagated. The ancient Europeans considered mistletoe to be the most magical and mysterious of all sacred plants and was thought to be the giver of life and fertility, a protector against poison, and an aphrodisiac. The mistletoe that grew on an oak tree was especially precious to the ancient Celtic Druids. White-robed Druid priests would cut the sacred oak mistletoe with a golden sickle, after which two white bulls would be sacrificed amid prayers that the recipients of the mistletoe would prosper. In the Middle Ages, mistletoe would be hung from ceilings to ward off evil spirits and placed over houses and stable doors to prevent witches from entering. Mistletoe has always been regarded as a sexual symbol and thought to have the power of bestowing fertility to those who would kiss under it.

A question comes to mind as to why we would want to glorify a plant that has the characteristics of Satan. If we think about it, Satan is like the moon. The moon doesn't have any power of its own to shine brightly, so it uses the power of the sun to shine but not nearly as bright as the sun, and the only time the moon shines is during the

ROBERT COOK

darker portion of a twenty-four hour day. In doing so, the moon mimics the sun. Satan, who also has no power of his own, has the ability to mimic God in that he is able to look like he has the power of God but doesn't, and in the future, he will again appear like he has great power.

All through history, everything he has done was to mimic God so he could suck the life out of all of God's creations that he could and leave them with nothing but eternal death. Satan is sin, and sin is poison to the soul. He comes to steal, kill, and destroy, and like Satan, mistletoe, which springs from dung, is a parasite that uses another organism's nutrients to sustain its own life and is worshiped as if it has power more than its creator. So how is it that we can celebrate life (Jesus) using something that is poisonous, is parasitic, has nothing at all to do with Christ, and represents death?

Another symbol of Christmas is the poinsettia plant; the ancient Aztec name for the plant is Cuetlaxochitl, which means "the flower of leather petals." They considered it to be a symbol of new life that could be earned by warriors who died in battle, who could return to earth as hummingbirds and sip the nectar of the poinsettia. The Spanish name for the poinsettia is *nochebuena*, which means "the flower of the holy night," and there is a legend attached to this name.

Long ago, a very poor little Mexican girl was desperate to give the Christ child a gift to show her love for him, but she had nothing to give nor did she have any money to buy a gift, so on Christmas Eve while she was walking to the church, she gathered some weeds from the side of the road. After she entered the church, she went to the altar and placed the weeds at the foot of the Christ child and they bloomed. From that point on, what we know of as the poinsettia were called the flowers of the holy night or the flowers of Christmas Eve. In America, we call this plant the poinsettia to honor Joel R. Poinsett, the first U.S. ambassador to Mexico during the early 1800s. While he was in Mexico, he took some cuttings from the plant and brought them back to his home to his greenhouse in South Carolina in 1826. The eighteenth-century Mexicans also came to believe that the plant was symbolic of the star of Bethlehem, and this is how the poinsettia became associated with the Christmas season.

The poinsettia is also used as an offering to a false goddess called the Virgin of Guadalupe. In 1531, a peasant Indian named Juan Diego was passing by a hill where there had been a temple built to worship the goddess of earth and corn whose name was Tonanzin and means "our mother." The temple was destroyed by the conquering Spaniards who forbid the indigenous people to pray to their protecting spirits. As he was passing by this place, he claimed to have suddenly become aware of a heavenly fragrance, and he could hear music, at which point he saw radiance like a glowing cloud, and then the image of Mary, the mother of Jesus, appeared dressed in blue, gold, and rose clothing. He said she urged him to return to the city and ask the bishop to build a shrine on the spot where the temple had been built. Eventually, she was given the name of the Dark Madonna and was embraced by the indigenous people. Today, her image can be found anyplace one can think of to look in Mexico: saloons, churches, homes, taxis, cradleboards, restaurants, jails, on the backs of t-shirts, and the list goes on and on. Her image adorned the flag of Don Miguel Hidalgo, who was the father of the Mexican independence movement. In the year 1754, she was declared the Empress of the Americas

ROBERT COOK

by a papal bull; the word *bull* is used to speak of an elaborate decree issued by a pope. In 1895, Pope Leo XII crowned her the queen of the Mexican people. In 1910, she was given the title of the Celestial Patron of Latin America, and in 1945, she was again crowned the Queen of Wisdom and of the Americas. In nearly every city or town in Mexico, there is a church consecrated to her name, and on the eleventh and twelfth of December, thousands of her faithful worshipers gather to give tribute to her, to petition her for a miracle, or to give thanks for one already received. When I went to Mexico on a mission trip, on every road everywhere we went there were these shrines along the side of the road; some were so small that one would have to get down on one's knees to see inside of the shrine, and some were big enough to walk into, and they all had candles one could light when a prayer was made, and they all had the image of Guadalupe inside. While I was there, I went into a Catholic church, and I saw a woman on her knees, praying before a priest under the image of Guadalupe. She is considered to be the mother of all Mexicans, the savior and helper of the indigenous spirit, the protectress of the poor, the ailing, and the dark. In Oaxaca, toddlers are dressed up to represent the many Indian tribes of Mexico and to look like Juan Diego. The children then pass through the church and leave their baskets of roses or poinsettias in reverence to the holy mother.

Why would we want anything to do with anything that has to do with any connection with the pagan worship and ritual of a false goddess who has been created and glorified by the imaginations of men? In other words, why would we have anything to do with anything connected to a man-made substitute for Christ?

Santa Claus:
Who Was He Really?

Saint Nicholas was born in Turkey during the second century, and he was a very pious person from a youth and gave his life to Christianity, becoming widely known for his compassion and generosity for the poor but was beheld by the Romans with contempt and was imprisoned and tortured for his faith. However, when Constantine converted to Christianity and became emperor of Rome, Saint Nicholas was freed and became a delegate to the Council of Nicaea in A.D. 325. He was known for his love of children and was designated the patron saint of children by the Roman church. It was Saint Nicholas that the Roman church used to meld together with the pagan god Odin to create who we now know of today as Santa Claus.

In the ninth century, the Roman creation was honored as King Frost by the Saxons of England. King Frost was represented by a man who would dress up with a fur hat or crown and would visit firesides. The Saxons believed that by welcoming winter as a deity or god, winter would be less harsh on them.

As the Vikings came to England during the last part of the ninth century and the early part of the tenth century, they brought with them their chief god whose name was Odin. They believed that Odin had twelve characters and the one for December was known as Jultid, which is where we get our word *Yuletide* or *Yule*. The Vikings believed that Odin visited earth in the month of December during the time of the winter solstice, and his companion was a raven or a crow. He would be disguised in a long, blue-hooded cloak, carrying a staff and a bag of bread, and would leave the bread as a gift at poor homesteads. The word Yule means "wheel," which is used to represent the sun. Yule was a German holiday that was dedicated to the birth of the sun god, which occurred in the dead of winter when the world has reached its darkest time of the year. The belief was that the darkness of the night before Yule lasted the longest and was just before the dawn. The holiday of Yule represented the world waiting on the rebirth of the sun. The celebration was held for twelve days, starting from December 21, which is generally accepted as the day of the winter solstice. The Yule and the Christmas celebrations had so many similarities that both Martin Luther and John Calvin both spoke out against the Christmas celebration, and the Puritans, who were the very first Europeans to settle in America, actually made it illegal to celebrate Christmas. During the Yule celebration, it was believed that it was possible to couple with the spirits of the dead and with demons who returned to the earth's surface.

Odin, whose name means "the inspired one," was a Norse god of the Swedes, Scandinavians, Germans, and Saxons, and so on. He was considered to be the god of victory, wisdom, magic, knowledge, poetry, and war. Human sacrifices would be made to him either before or after a battle. Those who were sacrificed to him were hung from trees, and suicide was considered to be an

ROBERT COOK

expectable shortcut to their heaven or what was known to them as Valhalla. Sacrifices would also be made to him if one wanted to change certain circumstances of life. He was depicted as a tall, old man with a white beard and wearing a cloak and rode the skies on his fast white horse with eight legs. He was believed to be a god who was a compulsive seeker of wisdom, who sacrificed one of his eyeballs to drink from the waters of the well of Mimir (the Norse representation of the source), after which he could see in the outward world with his normal eye and into the nether worlds with his blacked out eye, and the creation of the ancient Norse alphabet was attributed to him.

In the eleventh or twelfth century, a church was built to honor Saint Nicholas and became a site where believers would travel to spread his legend. In Germany, he was known as Saint Nikolaus and Sinter Klaas in Holland. In the Roman church, all designated saints have a feast day, and Saint Nicholas's feast day is on December 6, and on that day, gifts were given to children and to the poor to honor him. Today, many European people still celebrate his feast on the sixth of December, and some celebrate the Feast of Saint Nicholas only and do not celebrate Christmas. In fact my neighbor across the street from me does just that.

During the seventeenth and eighteenth centuries, the Dutch and German peoples crossed the Atlantic in great numbers and brought with them the legend of Sinter Klaas. In 1804, the New York Historical Society designated Saint Nicholas as their patron saint, who was known as the gift giver. Saint Nicholas Day dinner festivities featured a wooden image of Nicholas, who was thought of as being tall and wearing long robes. In 1812, a writer named Washington Erving, who had previously written a satirical book called *A History of New York*, revised his book, adding details about Nicholas/Santa Claus riding over the tops of trees in the same wagon or sled wherein he carried his presents for the children. For those who have seen the *Chronicles of Narnia*, the character known as Father Christmas looked nothing at all like the Santa Claus of today. He did have a white beard and long hair, but his cloths were not bright red with white furry trim, and he didn't have a big, wide black belt or a hat. His colors were a brick red, a dull gold or bronze and brown, his reindeer didn't fly across the tops of trees, and all of his gifts were inanimate objects that had magical powers, even a flask of liquid that had the power to bring back someone from the dead.

C.S. Lewis was born in Belfast in 1898, and the reason the Santa Claus in *The Chronicles of Narnia* looked like he did is because C.S. Lewis fashioned him after his conception of Santa Claus, which was also what the Europeans thought Santa Claus looked like. The image of Santa Claus continued to mutate but was not an established image in America until 1930 or 1931. Coca-Cola wanted to find a way to sell more coke during the winter months, so they commissioned a commercial illustrator named Haddon H. Sundblom, who had gone to work for Coca-Cola in 1924. He was asked to come up with something to promote more coke sales during the winter season because they would slump during that time. Consequently, from 1931 forward, with a new illustration every year for advertising purposes, the image of what was believed to be Santa Claus was transformed into that of a tall, robust, potbellied Santa Claus who was dressed in bright red velvet clothing with white fur trim, a wide black belt, and a hat with a fuzzy ball on the end of it, and whose eight reindeer could magically fly him, his sleigh, and his presents around the world in one night. This image was cemented in the public consciousness, and men like Norman Rockwell picked it up and ran with it, forever changing the image of an evil pagan Norse god into the warm fuzzy-wuzzy we now teach our children to look out for on the night before December 25 because he knows if they are good or bad. Some people have bought little elf dolls and place them in their children's room because the elf will report back to Santa if they are bad. Those parents will also move those elves around when that child is not in the room, which makes the child think that the little elf has its own power to move.

The Evergreen Tree:
What Was Believed About the Evergreen Tree?

The evergreen tree was and still is a favorite kind of tree to be used for idolatrous ritual, rites, and worship in the pagan world because it was believed that since the tree stayed green and never died during the winter that there was a god or a spirit living within it. The tree remained strong, green, and vibrant, even in the dead of winter, and where there were hard winters, the pagans felt compelled to appease the gods living within the trees in the hopes that these gods would help them. So the pagans would decorate these trees as a way of honoring the indwelling tree spirits. They would also place offerings of gifts at the foot of these trees, tokens of goodwill to please the god of the tree, as it were, and as an offering of appeasement to any evil spirits living in the trees.

Teutonic and Scandinavian peoples of northern Europe would decorate their houses and barns with the branches of evergreen trees to scare away demons. The Germanic peoples prized the evergreen tree because to them it was a sign of life in the midst of winter, and they would bring evergreen branches inside of their homes to give the tree dwelling spirits shelter.

Deuteronomy 16:21 says, "You shall not plant you a

grove of any trees near an altar of the Lord your God which you shall make" (KJV). In this verse and many more like it, the word *grove* has been used to replace the Hebrew word *asherah*, which comes from the root word *ashar*, which means "to be erect or to be upright," which is where the moral sense of uprightness or righteousness comes from. The *asherah* was called this because it was something that was set upright or erect in the ground and worshipped. The word occurs forty times in the Bible, and only by careful study can each passage give a correct view. Originally, the *asherah* was a living tree with the top cut off and the base fashioned into a certain shape or face to symbolize the tree of life and was an object of reverence and veneration, which was later replaced with a chiseled pillar of stone. The corrupted worship continued to greater depths of perversions until it became a form of lustful worship with a multitude of devotees involved in obscene orgies and lustful practices. We know from scripture that living trees were used in this form of pagan worship because in Exodus 34:13, God says "But you shall destroy their altars, break their images and cut down their groves/asherah" (KJV). If the *asherah* were made of stone, they would not have been able to cut them down, but they would have pulled or broken them down; only a tree could have been cut down. Again, in Deuteronomy 7:5, God says, "But this shall you deal with them; (the pagan nations) you shall destroy their altars, and break down their images, and cut down their groves/Asherah, and burn their graven images with fire" (KJV). In this verse, the words *break down* were used because they had images that were made of stone, and because the words *cut* and *burn* are used, we know that the *asherah* and the graven images were made of wood. Judges 6:25 tells

ROBERT COOK

Gideon to cut down the grove/asherah. In Jeremiah 10:1–5, God tells the children of Israel to listen to him and tells them, "Learn not the way of the heathen, and be not dismayed (confused) at the signs in the heaven; for the heathen are dismayed (confused) at them" (KJV). In this verse, the word *heathen* is used to speak of any nation or people who do not belong to the family of God who are practicing paganism. "For the customs (ordinances) of the people are vain: for one cuts a tree out of the forest, the work of the hands of the workman, with the axe. They deck it with silver and gold; they fasten it with nails and with hammers that it move not. They are upright as the palm tree, but speak not: they must needs be borne (carried) because they cannot go. Be not afraid of them; for they cannot do evil neither also is it in them to do good." In verse 4, the word *deck* means "to beautify an idol." So what God was telling his people is that he didn't even want them to do or even learn how to do any of the practices of the pagans for any reason because he didn't want his people influenced by them, and staying away from the practices of paganism still applies to day, as God has never said anything different. The rules of conduct set forth by God yesterday still apply today, some three or four thousand years later. Once again, one can color pagan worship and pagan ritual any which way one wants, but it is still paganism.

Whenever I talk to people about the pagan origins of most of the Christian holidays like Christmas, the single most common question people ask me is this, "Well, if we are doing it for the right reasons (to celebrate the birth of Christ), don't you think that it is okay?" First of all, the exact day of the birth of Christ is hidden from us because God, in all of his wisdom, didn't want us to celebrate the birth of Christ; otherwise, he would have given us an exact date of birth and instructions to celebrate his birthday, but he didn't, just as he gave us an exact record of the day of the death and resurrection of Jesus. The day of the birth of Christ was hidden from us because although it was a time to rejoice, the birth event was not nearly as important as his death and resurrection and just because it seems to be right in our thinking doesn't at all mean that God thinks the same way we do. It is, in fact, not the same way that God thinks about it, and God's Word says that we should not learn the ways or do the things that pagans do.

For the past two thousand years there have been many great men of God who have influenced and helped to shape the growth of the church and who have spoken out against these holidays, and the two most common reasons for their efforts to do away with these holidays is because they are not biblically sanctioned by God, and they all have pagan origins.

The Puritans were a people who worked to change society through religious and moral reforms but were persecuted and discouraged by the political struggles and man-made doctrines of the Church of England. They became convinced that the Church of England could not be reformed, so they packed their bags and came to America. The most famous of the Puritans was Oliver Cromwell, who was a statesman and a general who lead the parliamentary army to victory during the English civil war. Afterward, he took over England and declared himself "Lord Protectorate." Cromwell believed that it was his mission to cleanse the country of decadence. Before Cromwell, Christmas was celebrated with many of the traditional items like

ROBERT COOK

Christmas Day Mass, holly, evergreens, ivy and included nonstop dancing and singing, which was accompanied by nonstop consumption of alcoholic beverages, leading to drunkenness, promiscuity, gambling, and other forms of debauchery just as their pagan ancestors did before them but for a different reason at the same time of the year. The Puritans believed that Christmas was a pagan, wasteful festival that threatened the very core of Christian beliefs. They argued that nowhere in the Bible had God instructed his people to celebrate the birth of Christ, let alone with such debauchery. So in 1644, Cromwell enforced an act of parliament banning Christmas celebrations. In 1645, Parliament created the Directory of Public Worship, and accordingly, the population was to strictly observe Sundays as holy days and were not to celebrate or recognize any other festival days, including Christmas and Easter. Two years later, an ordinance was passed affirming the abolition of the feasts of Christmas and Easter.

The Puritans believed that the Bible was the true law of God, which provided a plan or philosophy on how one should live one's life. Their spiritual beliefs were strong, and since God was at the forefront of their minds, he was to motivate all of their actions, which resulted in their unity and the strengthening of their community. Because of the hardships of their pioneer life, this, in turn, made them sympathetic to the needs of one another. Their focus on the lordship of God and their resulting unity made their survival techniques more successful than other colonies to their south. The New Testament was their model and their devotion to live by; it was so great that it penetrated and filled their entire society. However, as with many religious societies, they went beyond that which the Word of

THE JERUSALEM CHURCH

God dictates in that they believed in the false doctrinal teaching of predestination and becoming too strict with their rejections of the things of the world, which turned into isolationism. With the negatives aside, the Puritans were the first to open a school that was free for all children in 1635, and four years later, the first American College was established and called Harvard in Cambridge. How about that? The Puritans were also the first to write books for children and to discuss the difficulties in communicating with them. While other Americans were taming our land from the east to the west, the Puritans were advancing our nation intellectually. After both the Puritans and the Pilgrims came to America, they saw Christmas as a pagan festival in origin and refused to participate in its celebration. So, as a result, Christmas was not considered to be a biblically sanctioned holiday from the arrival of the Pilgrims and English separatists in 1620 until 1870 when Christmas was declared a federal holiday. In Boston, Massachusetts, Christmas was outlawed from 1659 until 1681. Anyone missing work on December 25 would be fired, and factory owners would require their employees to come to work at 5:00 a.m. to ensure that they did not have time to go to church that day. Any student who failed to go to school on that day would be expelled, and on the day of the first Christmas under America's new constitution in 1789, Congress was in session. It was only after large numbers of the Irish and northern Europeans settled in America that Christmas become accepted in this country.

Great men of God like John Calvin, whose influence helped to shape the church as it grew, spoke out against the celebrating of Christmas, and so in 1537, Christmas passed without celebration under the insistence of Calvin. In 1541, after a period of exile from Geneva because of his beliefs, John Calvin once again began a campaign to abolish all nonbiblical holidays and achieved limited success in suppressing the feasts of the circumcision and the annunciation. Finally, in 1550, Calvin convinced the authorities in Geneva to outlaw Christmas and mandated that communion would only be celebrated on Sundays and not ever on superstitious pagan dates like December 25. John Calvin was a truly committed man of God who believed that Christmas was nonbiblical and an insult to God and once called those who honored the holiday rabid beasts. He wrote:

> I know how difficult it is to persuade the world that God disapproves of all modes of worship not expressly sanctioned by his word. The opposite persuasion which cleaves to them, being seated, as it were, in their very bones and marrow, is that whatever they do has in itself a sufficient sanction, provided it exhibits some kind of zeal for the honor of God. But since God not only regards (unsanctioned worship) as frivolous, but also plainly abominates, whatever we undertake from zeal to his worship, if at variance with his command, what do we gain by a contrary course? The words of God are clear and distinct. "Obedience is better than sacrifices." "But in vain they do worship me, teaching for doctrines the commandments of men" (Matthew 15:9, KJV).

Calvin also wrote this:

> The first evil here is, that an immense number of ceremonies, which God had by His authority abol-

ished, once and for all, have been again revived. The next evils, that while ceremonies ought to be living exercises of piety, men are vainly occupied with numbers of them that are both frivolous and useless. But by far the most deadly evil of all is, that after men have thus mocked God with ceremonies of one kind or other, they think they have fulfilled their duty as admirably as if these ceremonies included in the whole essence of piety and divine worship.

In other words, even though we think that because we are doing it for the right reasons, it is still a slap in the face of God, according to the Word of God. They attend these ceremonies and feel as if they have done well in the eyes of God when they have finished. But instead they have sinned against God by totally ignoring the whole essence of piety and the divine worship of God as instructed by their Creator.

Another great man of God was that Baptist preacher and healer of whom it is said once raised a man from the dead, whose name was Charles Spurgeon. Charles Spurgeon also spoke out against Christmas in one particular sermon named "Joy Born at Bethlehem," spoken from his pulpit on December 24, 1871. He said this:

We have no superstitious regard for times and seasons. Certainly we do not believe in the present ecclesiastical arrangement called Christmas; first, because we do not believe in the mass at all, but abhor it, whether it be said or sung in Latin or English; and secondly, because we find no scriptural warrant whatever for observing any day as the birthday of the Savior; and, consequently, its observance is a superstition, and not of divine authority.

ROBERT COOK

Spurgeon goes on to say that it was superstition that fixed the day of our Savior's birth to the twenty-fifth of December, and he was correct. Even though scripturally speaking, it is not possible to discover the true date of the birth of Jesus, and as I have said before, God has hidden the true birth date of Jesus from us. So why would we want to create a date to celebrate that which our God has actually purposely hidden from us?

Another great church reformist was John Knox, who also spoke out against the Roman church by contending that the true form of worship must be initiated by God. John Knox stood fast on Deuteronomy 12:32, which states that it is unlawful to add to or subtract from the worship that God instituted in his word. This means all religious ceremonies and institutions must have valid scriptural warrant if they are to be used to worship God and his Son. Which means that God will recognize and approve of only that which he has prescribed. Once during a public debate, John Knox said this:

> That God's word damns your ceremonies, it is evident; for the plain and straight commandment of God is, "Not that thing which appears good in your eyes, shall you do the Lord your God, but what the Lord your God has commanded you, that do you, add nothing to it; diminish nothing from it." (Deuteronomy 4:2) Now unless that you are able to prove that God has commanded your ceremonies, this His former commandment will damn both you and them.

With the Scottish reformation at full throttle, the Scottish church did away with a multitude of monuments of idolatry, such as graven images (statues of

Mary and other church-appointed saints), the Mass, false sacraments, and ecclesiastical holidays that were considered to be nonbiblical or pagan.

In 1560, John Knox and several other church leaders from the Scottish church put together the *First Book of Discipline* and the second paragraph reads like this:

> By contrary Doctrine, we understand whatsoever men, by Laws, Councils, or Constitutions have imposed upon the consciences of men, without the expressed commandment of God's word: such as be vows of chastity, foreswearing of marriage, binding of men and women to several and disguised apparels, to the superstitious observation of fasting days, difference of meat for conscience sake, prayer for the dead; and keeping of holy days of certain Saints commanded by men, such as be all those that the Papists have invented, as the Feasts (as they term them) of Apostles, Martyrs, Virgins, of Christmas, Circumcision, Epiphany, Purification, and other fond feasts of the Lady. (Mary) Which things in God's scriptures they neither have commandment nor assurance, we judge them utterly to be abolished from this Realm; (Scotland) affirming further, that the obstinate maintainers and teachers of such abominations ought not to escape the punishment of the Civil Magistrate.

Even the early American Presbyterians refused to celebrate Christmas and Easter and made those celebrations illegal according to church law. During the 1700s, the American Presbyterians used the Westminster Standards, which included a Directory of Worship and was first published in the year 1646. The Westminster

ROBERT COOK

Standards are a well-thought-out, scripturally based, and detailed summary of doctrinal beliefs and forms of worship with a biblically inspired, authentic faith of Christianity that through the guidance of God began to flourish during the sixteenth century Reformation and continued on through the seventeenth century.

The Directory for Worship was considered to be strictly in line with the Word of God when it came to the different forms of worship that were either commanded by God or considered holy by God. The early Presbyterian belief that the only biblically sanctioned holy day was the Sabbath, which Jesus commanded us to keep holy, was the basis for the Presbyterian Church's rejection of Christmas and Easter. They believed that the Word of God was the only infallible rule of faith and practice and no ritual or ceremony should take place in the worship of God that is not warranted in Scripture. They believed that the observances of so-called holy days that were not commanded by God had been found to interfere with the due sanctification of the Lord's Day, and adding to the appointments of God was superstition and was considered to have a negative impact on genuine obedience to the Word of God. Their most pointed objection was that experience had shown that the institution of holy days by human authority, no matter how pure the motive, invariably led to the disregard of the only Sabbath day instituted by God in the new testament.

For a full generation after the Civil War, the only denominations that recognized Christmas and Easter as God's holy days were the Episcopal and Lutheran churches. The rest of the Protestant churches, including the Baptists, rejected these holidays as pagan. They were not recognized as a day of any religious significance, and there was no reason or proof that Jesus was born on December 25.

Unfortunately, many of the major protestant denominations in America such as the Methodists, the Presbyterians, the Lutherans, and the Episcopalians of these days have gone far from their original stand on scriptural integrity and worship. Today, they embrace openly gay clergy, gay unions, gay Christians; these denominations are filled with pagan ritual and ideology. They have written new versions of the Word of God and re-written their by-laws so they conform to what they want to believe and how they want to live.

As time has moved forward, the fight against pagan man-made ritual and worship in the church has become faded. One of the last serious forms of opposition to these man-made holy days was in 1962 when the Counsel of the Free Presbyterian Church of Scotland issued a "Statement of Differences Between the Free Presbyterian Church of Scotland and Other Presbyterian Churches." It was a statement of many differences, but this is what it had to say about the observance of man-made holidays: "The Free Presbyterian Church rejects the modern customs becoming so prevalent in other Protestant denominations of the observing of Christmas and Easter." They saw these observances as a compromise to conform what was widely considered to be acceptable worship but totally unscriptural and reminded their brethren that all of these observances and festivals were all cast out of the church during the Scottish Reformation. They had objections to the many manger scenes and religious images that were erected in public places because these graven images were a blatant violation of the second commandment,

ROBERT COOK

which explicitly forbids the making of or using of any pictorial images or representations of God or Christ.

Here is a closer look at what Scripture says about the use of anything that is not sanctioned by God in the worship of God.

You shall not add to the word that I command you, neither shall you take away anything from it, that you may keep the commandments of your God which I command you" (Deuteronomy 4:2, KJV).

> Take heed for your selves that you are not snared by following them, after they are destroyed from before you; and that you ask not about their gods, saying, 'how did these nations serve their gods? Even so will I do likewise. You shall not do so unto the Lord your God: for every abomination to the Lord which He hates, have they done unto their gods, for even their sons and their daughters they have burnt in the fire of their gods. What thing so ever I command you observe to do it you shall not add to it nor subtract from it.
>
> Deuteronomy 12:30–32 (KJV)

God even requires us to purge even our language from the terminology of corrupt worship. "And in all things that I have said to you be careful and make no mention of the name of other gods, neither let it be heard out of your mouth" (Exodus 23:13, KJV).

As we can see from what the Bible says, we must be very careful not to be drawn into doing that which God has spoken out against and anything that is not scripturally ordained must be disregarded or shunned.

Another very common question I hear is, "Well, if

we are doing it for the right reasons, shouldn't it be acceptable to God?"

All questions can be answered using the Word of God. In the Bible, there is more than one example of one or more people who did what they thought was the right thing in the eyes of God but in fact did the wrong thing and paid an expensive price for their assumptions where God was concerned. "And Nadab and Abihu, the sons of Aaron, took either of them his censer and put fire therein, and put incense thereon, and offered strange fire before the Lord, which He commanded them not. And there went out fire from the Lord, and devoured them, and they died before the Lord" (Leviticus 10:1, 2, KJV). These young men assumed that what they did would please the Lord, but they were wrong. They didn't do exactly as the Lord had commanded them to do.

> And David and all Israel played before God with all their might, and with singing, and with harps, and with psalteries, and with timbrels, and with cymbals, and with trumpets, And when they came to the threshing floor of Chidon, Uzza put forth his hand to hold the Ark; for the oxen stumbled. And the anger of the Lord was kindled against Uzza and He struck him, because he put his hand to the Ark: and there he died before God.
>
> (1 Chronicles 13:8–10, KJV)

There is no doubt that Uzza was earnest in his efforts to keep the ark from toppling over off of the cart and onto the ground, and for a fact, he thought he was doing the right thing because if he knew he would be killed for putting his hand on the ark, he would not

ROBERT COOK

have done it. As we can see from verse 12, it scared David so badly when Uzza died that David wouldn't bring the ark into the city for fear that it would be the wrong thing to do.

By these scriptures, we know that just because we think that what we are doing is good in the eyes of God, doesn't mean that God is in agreement with us.

In Galatians 9:4–16, Paul rebukes the Galatians for backsliding into observing pagan rituals and worshipping pagan gods:

> But when the fullness of the time was come God sent forth His Son made of a woman, made under the law. To redeem them that were under the law, that we might receive the adoption of sons. And because you are sons, God has sent forth the Spirit of his Son into your hearts crying, "Abba, Father" wherefore you are no more a servant, but a son; and if a son, then an heir of God through Christ. How be it then when you knew not God, you did service to them which by nature are not gods. But now, after that you have known God, or rather known by God, how turn you again to the weak and beggarly (worthless) elements (rituals) where you desire again to be in bondage? You observe days, and months, and times, (observing pagan holidays and festivals by the lunar cycle) and years. I am afraid of you, that I have bestowed upon you labor in vain. Brethren, I beseech you, be as I am; for I am as you are: you have not injured me at all. You know how through infirmity of the flesh I have preached the gospel to you at the first. And my temptation which was in my flesh you despised not, nor rejected; but received me as an angel of God, even as Christ Jesus. Where

is then the blessedness you speak of? For I bear you record, that if it had been possible, you would have plucked out your own eyes, and have given them to me. (Here Paul was speaking of the level of their commitment to God and how it was so strong that they would have been willing to pluck out their own eyes before committing willful sin.) Am I therefore become your enemy, because I tell you the truth?

Now, we know for a fact that the Word of God speaks out against decorating trees, sunrise services, forty days of Lent, and many other forms of pagan worship and pagan ritual that we now do in the name of the worship of God. We know from both secular and religious historical records that the date of December 25 was a date assigned by men to worship pagan gods, as well as all of the other non biblically sanctioned Christian holiday dates, and from the Word of God and using a Jewish calendar that the birth of Jesus could have taken place only in the last part of September or the first part of October.

We must remember that when Jesus returns for his bride, she will be a perfect bride, which means that she will not be a bride that will be even slightly tainted by the smallest blemish of any paganism of any kind, which is what Paul gives us warning against in Colossians 2:16–23. "Let no man therefore judge you in meat, or in drink, or in respect of a holy day, (Ref. Leviticus 23) (KJV) or of the new moon, (Ref.1 Chronicles 23:31) (KJV) or of the Sabbath days: (All biblically sanctioned holidays) Which are a shadow of things to come; but the body of Christ. Let no man beguile (seduce) you of your reward in a voluntary humility and worship-

ROBERT COOK

ping of angels, intruding into those things which he has not seen vainly puffed up by his fleshy mind. And not holding the Head, from which all the body by joints and bands having nourishment ministered, and knit together, increases with the increase of God. Wherefore if you be dead in Christ from the rudiments of the world, why as though living in the world, are you subject to ordinances (pagan rituals) Touch not; taste not; handle not;(Speaking both materialistically and spiritually) Which all are to perish with the using after the commandments and doctrines of men? Which things have indeed a show of voluntary worship and humility, and neglecting of the body; not in any honor to the satisfying of the flesh.

So what can we conclude from all this information? I believe that God wants his people to go back to the basics. He wants us to go back to what his church was like during the first one hundred years of the Jerusalem church. He wants a church that is full of zeal, innocents, a church that is not steeped in pagan ritual, and that is being used to worship him. But most of all he wants his church to be as pure in heart, in our minds and our worship of him as it is possible for us to be and perfection is possible with Christ.

References

The Companion Bible–Authorized Version of 1611

The Strong's Exhaustive Concordance of the Bible

The Holman Bible Dictionary

The Dictionary of Early Christian Beliefs–A Reference Guide to the Doctrinal Beliefs of the Early Church Leaders for the First 300 years + of the Church. Edited by David W. Bercot.

The Brown-Driver-Briggs Hebrew and English Lexicon

The Thayer's Greek and English Lexicon

Answers.com

RealMagic.com

The Encyclopedia Wikipedia, an online encyclopedia

worldwide-festivals.com

oznet.ksu.edu

christianitytoday.com

penelope.uchicago.edu

biblcalholidays.com

goddessmystic.com

studytoanswer.net

ucgtp.org

earlychristianwritings.com

users.aristotle.net

ecole.evansville.edu

earlychurch.com

religionfacts.com

Justus.anglican.org

Iep.utm.edu

scrollpublishing.com

allaboutreligion.org

Epilogue

God created us to love us and to provide for us so that we might enjoy an intimate relationship with him. He wants us to recognize and worship him as our God and he gave us instruction on how he wants us to worship our God. There is no doubt that he wants our worship to be as pure in heart and mind as it is possible for us to be. He never wanted us to change what he had already instructed us to do and how we should do it. However we have changed his instructions by adding into our worship of him that which we thought would be a better and more acceptable way to worship our God. We have created new ways to worship him and all but done away with what he has instructed us to do.

So within the pages of this book are the history both secularly and biblically of our religious holy days and how we came to worship our God in the way we do now. You will find here that things are not quit like we think they are and you will see how our God truly feels about what we have done to his instructed methods of worshipping him. It is a guarantee that what you will find here in this book will be very interesting indeed.

With Many Blessings to You
Robert P Cook